Lost Souls: FOUND!

Inspiring S...

Kyla Duffy and ....ord

Published by Happy Tails Books™, LLC

Happy Tails Books™ uses the power of storytelling to affect positive change in the lives of animals in need. The joy, hope, and (occasional) chaos these stories describe will make you laugh and cry as you embark on a journey with their authors, who are guardians and/or fosters of rescued cats. "Reading for Rescue" with Happy Tails Books brings further awareness to animal advocacy efforts. Additionally, each sale results in a financial contribution to animal rescue groups.

Lost Souls: Found!™ Inspiring Stories About Cats by Kyla Duffy and Lowrey Mumford

Published by Happy Tails Books™, LLC www.happytailsbooks.com

© Copyright 2011 Happy Tails Books™, LLC. Printed and bound in the United States of America. All Rights Reserved. No part of this book may be reproduced in any form or by any electronic or mechanical means, including information storage and retrieval systems, without written permission from the publisher.

The publisher gratefully acknowledges the numerous cat rescue groups and their members, who generously granted permission to use their stories and photos.

The following brand names are registered trademarks and the property of their owners. The author and publishing company make no claims to the logos mentioned in this book including: Petfinder.com, PETCO, Petsmart, Velcro, Mustang GT, Paypal

Photo Credits (All Rights Reserved by Photographers):

Front Cover: *Wolfie*, Ashley Johnson, www.lovemuttphotography.com
Back Cover Top: *Sloan*, April Turner, www.uturnstudios.com
Back Cover L: *Molly*, Stephanie Smith, www.pawsitivelypictures.com
Back Cover Mid: *Peanut*, Ashley Johnson
Back Cover R: *Jerry*, Ashley Johnson
Inside Title: *Riley*, April Ziegler, www.aprilziegler.com

Publishers Cataloging In Publication

Lost Souls: Found!™ Inspiring Stories About Cats/ [Compiled and edited by] Kyla Duffy and Lowrey Mumford.

p. ; cm.

ISBN: **978-0-9826964-1-5**

1. Cats. 2. Cat rescue. 3. Cats – Anecdotes. 4. Animal welfare – United States. 5. Human-animal relationships – Anecdotes. I. Duffy, Kyla. II. Mumford, Lowrey. III. Title.

SF426.5 2011
636.8   2010915176

Cat Rescue Resources:

Alley Cat Allies (Great resource for feral cat help)
http://www.alleycat.org/

Blind Cat Rescue
http://www.blindcatrescue.com/

Paws For Life
http://www.pawsforliferescue.org/

RescueCats Inc.
http://www.rescuecats.org/

Rocky Mountain Siamese Rescue
http://www.co.siameserescue.org/

Texas Siamese Rescue
http://www.tx.siameserescue.org/

Want more information about the cats, authors, and rescues
featured in this book? http://happytailsbooks.com

Contents

Introduction:
When Adoption Isn't an Option

I was introduced to Paws for Life Rescue and Adoption (PFL) by a friend who volunteered for them. I was not looking for a rescue to join, but I went to a few adoption events and realized that working with PFL was something I wanted to do. I began by fostering one cat. Since then I have fostered nearly 50 dogs, cats, puppies, and kittens and helped at numerous adoption events. I also transport animals to their new homes and vet appointments when needed. Some of these animals were sick or injured, which required medical care and time to recuperate; most of them were scared and unsure.

Sharon, a woman who knows I'm a rescue volunteer, told me about a feral cat in her neighborhood. She had been feeding the cat for about a year but could not continue doing so. Additionally, the cat now had two kittens.

Sharon asked if there was anything we could do for this cat family. We considered a live trap, but knowing that the door could potentially hurt the kittens when they followed their mom in, Sharon instead set up a cat cage on her patio. She strung a line from the door of the cage through her kitchen window and then waited to trap the cats at feeding time. When the cats went inside the cage to eat, she pulled the string and shut the door behind them. She managed to catch the mother and both her kittens.

I went with two other volunteers to retrieve the cats. As we were leaving Sharon's house, we noticed another two kittens hiding under a car a few houses away. The volunteers were able to catch these two abandoned kittens, too. PFL altered and vaccinated all the cats.

The four kittens in this story were socialized and adopted, but the mother had to remain outdoors because she would never be tame enough to become an indoor pet. This is typical example of many feral cats. The process we used to help the mother cat is commonly referred to as TNR (trap, neuter, return), in which a feral cat is humanely trapped, neutered and vaccinated, and then returned to its neighborhood. After the feral is returned, he or she needs a human caretaker to provide basic shelter, food, and water. In this case, we sent the mom to live on a farm where she could be properly cared for because her previous caretaker was no longer available.

Usually a caretaker provides for a feral "colony," not just a single cat, as groups of ferals tend to stick together.

The caretaker establishes a feeding schedule and watches the colony for injured or sick cats or new arrivals to the neighborhood. This approach reduces disease, the chances of starvation, and the effects of harsh weather on the colony. It also controls the population and eliminates fighting and yowling caused by mating.

Luckily I had the resources of PFL, a group of dedicated volunteers who rescue homeless animals in the Metro Detroit area, to help with the cats from Sharon's neighborhood. Like many other rescues around the country, PFL adopts out feral cats who can be socialized, and those who can't are spayed/neutered and released.

Whether I help place a cat or kitten in a forever home with a family, or I help TNR a feral cat to live in a colony, I find animal rescue very rewarding. From the stories in this book, you'll see that I'm not alone. There are many satisfying ways to help cats in need. The stories in this book highlight some examples: from simply adopting your next pet to volunteering to transport needy cats from shelters to rescues or new homes, the ways you can make a difference in cats' lives are endless.

If these stories inspire you to "take paws" and think about how you can lend a hand to help needy cats, this book has been a success. Through careful feral colony management, a commitment to adopting subsequent pets, and people's generous donations of time and money to local shelters and rescues, we *will* see a day where there are no longer hungry, unloved, homeless cats roaming our streets.

 *Cassie Reich*

Inspiring Stories About Cats

Who saves whom, I wonder. Bereft from the loss of my 18-year-old Siamese two years ago, I finally couldn't continue in a furless household any longer, so I visited the Rocky Mountain Siamese Rescue website and wondered if one of the little bundles of fur I saw there could be my new four-legged love. I adopted a very busy, three-month-old little boy, Gem, and he has filled the house with his enormous personality, affection, and warmth. I am saved. Gem is also the perfect model for my pet portrait oil painting. -*Susan Becker*

Christmas Spirit

I slammed the door against the cold, letting out my breath in a puff of whiteness. Sniffling, I kicked off my boots and scuffled across the floor in my fuzzy wool socks to hang up my coat. It was just after shoving my scarf into its place that I saw him, staring forlornly through the back door with his wide-set green eyes. His runny pink nose was pressed against the glass, his whiskers buffeted by the icy wind. The white fur on his paws was tinged with brown, and seated on the hard cement, he looked scrawny. When he saw me, he scampered timidly away, his tail disappearing into the bare branches of our back yard. Nevertheless, I poured some dry cat food into a bowl and slipped it out the door in case he returned.

I began to see him regularly, either pressed up against a wall or huddled in a corner, trying to avoid the rapidly deteriorating weather. Each time my mother or I put out food, he edged a little closer, drawn toward the warmth and safety of our house. My mom was itching to do more for him, but we already had two cats and were busy enough with Christmas shopping, school, and work.

Still, the day came when we had to decide how committed we were to our unfortunate visitor. It was bitterly cold, and the gray sky hinted at a coming storm. As my mom slid open the door to put out a dish of food, the tomcat scurried in. He was shivering and thin, his ribs faintly visible under his skin. He buried his snout in the food, and my bewildered mom shut the door quietly behind him.

Mom tempted the cat into the bathroom, where he could be kept separate from our other cats, and he submitted easily to using the litter box. He gobbled up every morsel of food we gave him, and after his first indoor night, he looked a little cleaner and a lot happier. I called him Linus because of his easygoing nature, my fondness for Charlie Brown, and the prevailing holiday spirit. He didn't try to escape the bathroom, and when our other cats snuffled under the door and hissed territorially, he only mewled, lowering his head to smell them back.

We took Linus to the vet a few days later to confirm what we already knew: he was an unaltered male, about a year old, and he didn't have fleas. He sat patiently through his shots and vaccinations, almost as though he knew they would do him good. Linus purred when we stroked his nose through the bars of the cat carrier, his whole chest rumbling as I scratched him behind the ears. He was an absolute sweetheart.

Linus was introduced to our other cats just a few days after he was neutered. When they batted him on the head and sniffed him cautiously, he merely submitted, acknowledging that while he was almost twice their size, he was the newcomer, the odd one out. Linus quickly befriended our cats, letting the younger one rub against his belly and tumbling with them across the furniture in pretend fights. He never struck out, didn't hiss, and walked down the stairs like a baby: one step at a time. We called him the Zen Kitty; he spent a lot of time sleeping and ate with a slow deliberateness.

It didn't take long for us to love Linus. At first we'd thought of putting him up for adoption, but as soon as it was clear that he got along with our cats, we claimed him as our own. He was too distinguished to give up, and our determination to keep him was only made stronger when our one feeble attempt to give him to a family friend fell through. We had never really wanted to give Linus away anyway. One frosty morning, as I tumbled downstairs to find him curled up on the couch next to our kitten, it was clear: Linus had already found his family.

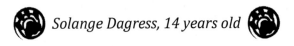 *Solange Dagress, 14 years old*

Enough to Share

L ia-Belle had been starved, abused, and over-bred. When she was confiscated by authorities that summer day a decade ago, she weighed just over three pounds. The backyard breeder, from whom Lia had been confiscated, admitted to the court that she set out food and water for the 54 Siamese cats and 15 Alaskan Huskies only twice a week. Consequently, the animals had to fight each other for basic nourishment.

After I adopted her, we discovered Lia had also suffered a tear in her diaphragm, most likely the result of having been kicked. A 10-year-old classic Siamese, Lia weighed less than half of what she should have. After doing Lia's spay, the rescue's vet said that Lia had the most "used" uterus he'd ever seen; as if she'd been bred for every possible litter. That's an estimated three-to-five kittens per litter, three times a year, for approximately 9½ years—totaling between 85 and 140 kittens!

Lia gained some weight while being held as evidence, and she gained a little more while at the rescue from which I adopted her. When she joined Kenishi (Nish) and me in Boston later that fall, she discovered that she only had to share food with one other cat, that food came twice a day, and that there was *always* kibble in the gravity feeder that holds 1½ pounds at a time. When your issue is starvation, and you have finally been fed, both literally and figuratively, there's an overwhelming desire to territorialize that which feeds you. For Lia, that translated into eating everything that didn't eat her first, wasn't nailed down, and couldn't be pried up.

Lia would lay her body over her dish and eat with Nish from his bowl. Then, when his was empty, she would go back to her own dish. What was hers was hers, and what was *his* was hers. She would routinely grab food and carry it off. Lovingly, I referred to these as Little Lia TV Dinners. When I came in from grocery shopping, she would study my unpacking of the cat food cans with her lower jaw moving ever-so-slightly, as if she was counting them to herself—I really believe she *was* counting. It makes sense to me that animals have some means by which they count the noses of their young, and she'd certainly had a lot of noses to count.

Sometimes I'd see Lia get on her hind legs and open that cupboard's door, and I often found it open. It seemed to me that she was checking to make sure there was more food. A part of me wondered if she also did subtraction. She studied everything I did. She was like Velcro and very much became a "Meowma's girl." But, mostly, she hung out by her food dishes, and for her first three years with me, Lia ate incessantly. She once even managed to empty the gravity feeder. Even the surgical removal of nearly two pounds of new-found blubber didn't hold her back from steadily gaining weight and eventually reaching a top weight of 14 pounds.

You can't actually sit your cats or dogs down and ask them to share how they feel or tell you what they need; you can only observe and look for patterns and habits, looking for any deviations. Sometimes the changes are subtle, and other times they are tossed right in front of you. This particular July had been unusually hot, so hot that the only one doing any eating was Lia, and even she was eating lightly. When the heat wave finally broke, and Da Kids, as I called them, were starting to move away from the A/C, I noticed that Nish had really thinned down. He also appeared to be in pain. He'd been diagnosed with the early stages of chronic renal failure just before Lia's adoption and had responded well to prescription food. I took him to see Doc Sawyers, who ran an updated kidney blood panel. Nishi was crashing. He spent a few days with Doc, and when it looked like he was rebounding, I was able to take him home after learning how to give him subcutaneous fluids. Nish parked himself in the leopard-print, beanbag-like "pouf" chair, and that, pretty much, is where he stayed.

For the next week I woke early, so I could hand-feed Nish and give him fluids before going to work. He seldom left the pouf chair, but I nevertheless set out dishes of food and water for him in case he did. When I got home, I did it all again. True to her character, Lia studied my care of Nishi like she was preparing for an exam. She seemed to understand that he needed the attention this time, much like she had after her surgeries. Then, he had checked in on her seemingly every hour like a trained nurse doing rounds. This time she kept an eye on him.

It was our new routine, and it's what I expected the evening I discovered that Lia had been carrying food to Nishi while I was away at work. I was already feeling emotionally drained because Nish clearly wasn't rebounding as well as hoped. I got in after work and gave myself a few minutes to just sit down before starting his sub-Q line and putting my fingers into the wet food to hand-feed him.

Sitting on the couch, my right hand dropped beside me, and I felt wetness. Oh, great! My first thought was that Nish had gotten out of the pouf chair, gone as far as the couch, and urinated right there. That would not be a good sign. I went to the kitchen to get the paper towels, and when I returned to the living room, in the waning sunlight I saw scattered reflections of wetness forming a path from where Nishi sat in the pouf chair, down the couch, onto the floor, and up to the food dishes. It resembled the residue that was usually left from the Little Lia TV Dinners...and then it occurred to me that it *was* the residue from food I'd left out for Nish earlier that day. Lia had been carrying it to him while I was gone. Just as he had looked out for her, she was looking out for him.

It was the most beautiful thing I'd ever seen. Not only was theirs a picture of one life caring for another, but it also represented Lia's confronting and rising above her greatest fear—hunger—as she was able to share her food with another. We lost Nishi shortly thereafter, but that selfless act seemed to have affected Lia, too, because she became less territorial about her food dishes. She finally rested between feedings. In every way, it seemed that her fears had been replaced by trust. She may not have been able to put it into words, but Lia is proof that life changes as much as you are willing to change with it, a concept she obviously learned well.

 *Susan Reimers*

A Happy Survivor

After work I climbed the 36 steep rock steps to the deck of my house in the remote mountain area west of Estes Park, Colorado. Nearby I saw the resident fox waiting, protecting his den on the hillside behind the house, hopeful for after-dinner scraps to feed to his kits. The chipmunks scattered as usual, the birds fluttered around the feeders, and a new visitor was hanging around this evening—a handsome but terribly thin cat, who ran and hid as I approached. As he bolted, I could see his ribs sticking out. For how long had he been starving?

When I reached the top step, I stood on the deck and looked out at the surrounding beauty of the Roosevelt National Forest. Despite the coyotes howling in preparation for their evening hunt, it was a peaceful moment with sweet deer grazing nearby. Then I again saw the stray cat, whom I would soon name Jack. He peered around the corner of the cabin at me. I already had two female cats in the house and certainly didn't need another, but it was October, the weather was getting colder, and well, I'm a sucker!

I fed Sophie and Phoebe their dry kibble. Then I took a bowl outside and sat on the deck. Sophie and Phoebe meowed at the door, probably wondering why they were not allowed out. They didn't know about the foxes and coyotes that were looking for a tasty meal. Soon enough, Jack came near. He carefully approached me while I talked softly to him. It didn't take long for him to curl up in my lap, purring loudly and enjoying his dinner.

As much as I tried, he did not want to come inside that night. My heart ached as I worried about him being outside alone. The next morning I put more food out, and as I stood watching, the fox attempted to take his food. I shouldn't have worried—Jack shooshed him away and happily ate his breakfast!

Like I said, it was October. October in the Rocky Mountains is cold and unpredictable, so I was glad that a few nights later I was able to coax Jack into the house. Both my girls accepted him right away. He purred loudly and was clearly appreciative of a warm home and a good meal.

My husband was working out of town when Jack adopted me, but he had already grown used to my need to "rescue" pets. When my husband called the night Jack came inside, I told him, "We have a new cat." He said, "I knew it!"

It was obvious that Jack had been someone's beloved pet, so we posted signs at the ends of our dirt roads. Some people called, but no one described a cat like Jack, so he became ours.

Our Jack was a mere 13 pounds when we rescued him with his bones poking out, but now, years later, he is a healthy, happy 23 pounds. I often wonder if some family out there is missing him or wondering about him, but despite our efforts, no one has ever claimed him. That's sad for them because Jack is wonderful! He is the love of our lives. He purrs louder than any cat I have ever known.

Recently our sweet, brave Jack surprised us yet again. We moved to another remote mountainous area, taking Jack and the others with us. Here Jack enjoys hunting mice, proudly leaving them at the doorway each morning. One day in September our mountain community was turned upside down by the Reservoir Road Fire. Sadly, Jack and his kitty siblings were too frightened to come to us when we were forced to evacuate with flames raging close behind. Two of our cats were rescued by firefighters that first day, but Jack remained missing.

A few days later we were allowed to visit our home for a short time to gather important things and assess damage. While my husband gathered our belongings, I combed the ash-covered hills, calling for Jack.

We were only allowed 30 minutes at the house before being escorted back down, as it was still unsafe for residents to be there. So when Jack didn't respond, I sat on the steps and began to cry. Then, suddenly, I heard a faint meow. I listened carefully and heard it again. There, crawling out from under some burnt timber was my Jack! I picked him up, hugged him, and cried! He quickly began to purr, and I knew all was well with the world again.

Today, Jack and the rest of the family are safely back at home. Jack still purrs louder than any cat I have ever known, and tonight I fall asleep peacefully knowing my happy Jack is next to me. He's happy and so are we!

 *Shereen Raucci*

Last Wish Fulfilled

One night Nanette from RescueCats called. The police department was asking us to take in a few cats. It seems a man had taken his own life and the note he left stated his cats were to go to a no-kill rescue. Nanette had taken in the cats, but there was one black-and-white tuxedo cat who wouldn't let anyone touch him and wouldn't eat.

I have always been good with cats who have behavioral issues, so she thought I might have some insight. I drove down to the rescue and found Nanette sitting in front of the kitty's condo. He was pacing up and down, growling, and hissing. He wouldn't allow anyone near the condo.

I wasn't sure exactly what I was going to do but remembered a story my mom had told me. She had inherited a Boston Terrier, Tiny, from my aunt when she passed away.

Tiny refused to eat and just moped around, so Mom called the vet. He told her that animals understand much more than we know and that she needed to explain to Tiny that Aunt Pauline had passed away and that she would see her again one day, but in the meantime, Mom would be caring for her, feeding her, and loving her in just the same way Aunt Pauline did. Mom was skeptical but went home, sat down, and talked with Tiny, exactly as the vet had advised. Believe it or not, Tiny started eating and was perfectly fine from then on.

Taking this story into consideration, I sat down in front of this cat and started talking to him. I told him that his owner could not stand the pressure of this world any longer, but his last wish was that his cats were looked after and loved and that nothing bad was to happen to them. I told him that we were going to love him, feed him, and care for him until we found him a forever home. I told him that his owner had loved him very much and would be waiting for him when the time came, but until then, we would love him and take care of him.

As I was talking, the cat's pacing slowed, and he finally sat down in front of me and let me scratch his chin. At that point, a strange feeling came over both Nanette and me, a warm feeling like something was washing over us and through us. We both broke down in tears. It was so intense that Nanette had to leave the room.

The only explanation I can think of is that this man's spirit had stayed with his favorite cat until he was sure all the cats were in good hands, and the feeling we felt was him letting go of this world, knowing that his last wish was fulfilled.

 *Sherry Davis*

The Spare Cat

We used to put inexpensive dry cat food out on our deck for the local raccoons and opossums, alongside trays of seeds and goodies for the chipmunks, mice, and other small neighborhood wildlife. One evening we noticed an orange tabby cat sneaking a snack at the cat food tray. As soon as he spotted us, he bolted. Clearly he wasn't too interested in people.

His visits to the tray became a daily event, so we took care to make sure there was always food there for him. We had to be cautious in observing him; even seeing us through the glass door was enough to send him scurrying for cover, though he didn't seem to be at all put off by the resident cats watching him through the glass. He looked to be in pretty good shape: perhaps a once-loved pet now homeless and fallen on hard times.

As time wore on, the cat stopped running when we appeared by the door and would even stay, warily, while one of us stuck a hand through the door with a cup of food for a refill. It was about then we started referring to him as the spare cat, as in, "The spare cat's here, did you put out food?" We'd look at the spoiled resident cats and remind them, "You better behave: We have a spare cat who can replace you."

A few more weeks passed, and the spare cat now not only allowed us to pet him, he insisted on it! He seemed to prefer my partner, Cj, at first, and would sit and meow until she came out to scratch his ears while he ate.

If we were gone, he'd watch for us and come running when he heard the car pull into the driveway, rolling and purring in greeting as we got out. We'd already decided that should he warm up enough to us to want to come in, we'd be happy to give this spare cat a home. I'd even called the vet to arrange a no-appointment drop-off for checkup, testing, shots, and neutering any time we were able to capture him. The spare cat had only to take us up on the offer.

Finally it happened. I opened the door to refill the tray, and he strolled right through like he knew he belonged. We encouraged him and urged him on, until he got close enough and allowed me to pick him up. He spent the night in isolation from the other cats and was off to the vet first thing in the morning.

The spare cat now answers to Spare, and we don't see any real need to change it. Better the spare cat than the homeless cat, no? The vet declared him very healthy, gave him a round of vaccinations and a neutering, and Spare came home to stay.

Spare is the calmest, most Zen cat we've ever met. He's loving and openly affectionate, even to the dogs, and spare or not, he has made himself totally at home.

There is a legend that a Buddhist monk, after several incarnations of service and devotion, is allowed to take one lifetime "off," a vacation if you will, and return for that lifetime as a cat, spending a few years just relaxing, dozing in the sun, and doing as he pleases, before returning to another lifetime as a monk. I would have thought it merely a legend until Spare came along. I look into those calm, serene, ancient yellow eyes, not too different from the color of a monk's saffron robe, and I believe it is quite possible.

Spare takes care of us as much as we take care of him. He seems to know when we're hurting, emotionally or physically; he will come and curl up on our chests, his breastbone aligned with ours, purring us back to feeling better. His gentle, loving spirit has been felt and noted by other people, too, so it's not just us. Everyone should be so lucky as to have a Spare cat around the house.

 *Kyla Jones*

Kitty Kwips

Can't Capsize Cat: Dave lived with his cat on a small boat in the Virgin Islands. Like most locals, he was used to storms and determined to ride out the coming hurricane. But when the folded sails tore away from the mast of his boat in the mounting storm, Dave knew he had to get himself and his kitty to shore. Taking a crated cat in his small dinghy would be unsafe because if it capsized, his cat would most likely drown. Instead, Dave stripped off his shirt and shoes, grabbed a handy roll of duct tape, and taped the struggling cat to his chest. He back-stroked 100 yards to the pier through roiling water and torrential rain, dodging the debris of damaged boats and buildings and keeping the terrified cat above water as much as possible. At last, exhausted, he and the cat made it to shore and shelter. They survived and lived together for many years thereafter. As he tells the story, Dave's eyes mist up, and he says, "That was the best cat I ever had." -*Crystal Wood*

Over the Right Fence: On my children's walk home from the bus stop, they encountered a kitten with a terribly swollen eye. Without hesitation, we scooped her up, put her in a carrier, and raced her to the vet, who was 19 miles away. She was diagnosed with an ulcerated cornea. You could actually see the large hole in her cornea! My daughter thought she knew who owned the kitten, but when she called to tell them we had the kitten, they responded, "Just throw her over the fence." Ha! We named her Margaret, and she has been such a sweetie. We are so glad to have her with us. -*Andi Anderson*

Feed the Soul

D ay after day, there he sat: the big, gray cat on the top step at the back door, staring into the house. I told him, "Go home," but every day he just looked back at me and didn't move.

Each morning he'd be there on the top step, saying with his eyes, "I am yours now."

I blame our finally acquiring Forest Kitty on the fact that I'm a Southern woman. Of course, all Southern women know one thing, even if they don't know anything else (or if they can't do anything else): When someone or something comes to your house, you feed it. Food is always a good strategy, as it can buy time, serve as a distraction, or solve a world of ills. As the descendent of a long line of Mother Earth-type Southern women, I could only hold out for a few days with the sad grey kitty sitting and pleading on the steps to come in. And so, with just one bite of food, Forest Kitty became ours...forever.

We named him "Forest Kitty," as he simply wandered into our lives out of the forest surrounding our 25 acres of land. Upon arrival he was a full-fledged tomcat, so we took care of that first, got his shots up to date, and he became one of our little "herd" of four cats, two dogs, and two horses. Yep, we're true animal lovers and hairball managers.

Chunk, as we've taken to calling him, has decided he likes the indoor life. We fondly call him Chunk because, well, he is built like a Chunky bar. He is big, solid, and strong, with long claws and girth, weighing in at about 15 pounds. He has a good (a.k.a. lazy) attitude toward most of the other animals with the exception of one. Both Chunk and the other male cat, Blackie, couldn't stand our little tortie, Opal, but the two of them are best buddies, enjoying daily wrestling matches, dirt wallowing, and timed tree climbing. Chunk will tolerate the enthusiasm of our six-month-old Golden Retriever, but he lets her know who is boss, and he is always clear about when he is tired of playing.

Chunk, living up to his name, particularly enjoys lounging for long days in my recliner by the fire. Then, at about dusk, he'll ask to go out, so he can sleuth around to catch a mouse, mole, or vole. One morning I stepped barefoot onto the deck, right upon what was left of his "conquest." I did a really innovative little hip-hop/Latin/Native American dance thing around the back porch trying to get the mouse parts off of the bottom of my foot. I think that morning I actually developed a new "Dancing with the Stars" category!

Obviously, Chunk does have his drawbacks, but then, he *is* a cat.

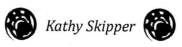

Kathy Skipper

A Teaspoon of Courage

This is a story of great loss, great joy, and a teaspoon of courage. After having Mr. Max and Miss Mattie, yellow tiger-striped littermates, since they were six weeks old, we lost Mattie to cancer when she was 10. Max was so lonesome that he would go through the house calling out for her.

Three weeks after Mattie was euthanized, I came home and found Max sitting at the bottom of the stairs wailing. He was so distraught he wouldn't even come upstairs for his treat, a ritual we had since he was a kitten. That night, as with many of the nights since her passing, Max woke me with his wailing.

I knew he needed a brother. Since he was an older cat, I began searching our local human society's web page for a young adult, thinking an adult would be most compatible. I decided to adopt another yellow tabby. There were pictures on the website of male tiger cats, so I set out the next morning to adopt a brother for Mr. Max.

I soon found out that the adult yellow tabbies had already been adopted. Great news for them; not so good for Max and me. I began looking at the kittens. I spotted one who was a bit scrawny and obviously scared. He was funny looking because his whiskers had been chewed off. That would be enough to scare any cat! I asked to see him, and we were escorted to a visiting room. The staff warned me that he was skittish, and they didn't think he would make a good pet. They told me he had been found as a stray and suggested I meet with other friendlier kittens, but I wanted to meet this little yellow fella and find out if he needed me (and Max). I was pretty sure we needed him.

Once in the visiting room, I sat down on the floor and let the kitten walk around and get used to me. Eventually I began to stroke him as he wandered past. He didn't respond immediately, but he didn't try to run away, either. When I picked him up, I could see that he had dried tar on his front paws. They were no longer sore, but I winced at the pain he must have been in when that happened. I could also see that there was dirt in both ears. Just six weeks old—what a scary life he must have led before finding his temporary home. He was also very small for his age.

After our time together, I began to fall in love with the little kitten. He only warmed up to me a little, but I was sure he just needed some TLC. So I named him Mr. Willson and took him home.

The only question in my mind was whether Max was ready to meet Willson. Was bringing home a scared, skittish kitten the remedy Max needed? Of course it was; Max just didn't know it yet.

When we got home, I set up a spot for Wills in the bathroom thinking he would be comfortable in a small space as he transitioned into his new, permanent home. I held him for a few minutes and then kenneled him for about an hour. I had not introduced him to Max yet, but Max knew he was there by his scent.

After an hour I checked on him; he had settled into his bed. I thought that was a good sign. I picked him up and sat with him. Max watched from a distance but didn't try to approach us. I held Willson for about an hour and then put him back in his room.

It was as if Max sensed that Willson was special from the start. Max watched as I held him, not seeming jealous or anxious. Eventually, Willson began to notice Max and watch him. However, he didn't attempt to investigate who he was.

Sunday evening I opened the bathroom door and let Willson check out the living room. He slowly walked out, and Max met him just outside the door. They sniffed and walked sideways toward each other—as only cats can do—and then Max let out just one hiss. Willson cowered, but rather than running back into the bathroom, he ran to me. Victory!

Willson was timid, but he took to me. I continued to kennel him in the bathroom because I wasn't sure how he and Max would do when they were left alone. After 10 days, one afternoon I came home to find Max sitting in front of the bathroom door meowing, talking to Willson. I decided they were ready to get to know each other better and began allowing Willson more freedom.

To my surprise, Max started playing with Willson. In due course, rather than Willson sneaking up and pouncing on Max, Max began to sneak-attack Willson. Max even let Willson snooze with him in his favorite chair. A success story? Yes, but...

The humane society staff was certain that Willson would never make a good pet because he was so skittish, and in a way they were right. He got over his nervousness with Max and me, but noises were another thing. People's voices sent him to the furnace room. He quickly learned that a ringing doorbell meant another human was coming, and he had to move quickly. He would fly to the steps and hit the furnace room before I could get to the door.

Courage. Willson needed courage, but how could I give that to him? Over time and with encouragement, he gradually got a bit braver. He will peer from the top of the stairs before determining if it was safe to venture farther if someone comes and stays a while. A few chosen people, such as my niece Katie and my friend Tracy, have since been privileged to pet Willson. And when I go out of town and Jo Ellen stays with him, he becomes quite chummy with her, although he gives her the cold shoulder after I return home.

Regret? Absolutely not! Wills is a delightful, happy cat who is attentive and loving. When I think what might have happened to him if I had not saved him, I worry for other shy guys like him. His first weeks of life were not the best, but his life now is full of joy.

Since we lost Max when Willson was two, he is now the big brother to Spencer. Spencer, a 12-week-old yellow tabby, joined our family six months after Max's passing. While Max taught Willson to be a good big brother, Spencer taught Willson one big lesson about courage. Spenc loves to jump onto the banister and walk it. Wills watched him do this day after day. He wanted to try it but was afraid. He would sit at the banister and meow for me to set him up there. Then, one day he had the courage to jump up by himself.

Even with Willson's new-found courage, Spenc knows he has to stay out of Will's way when the doorbell rings.

 *Mary Jo Kenneally*

A Cat Named Sue

arly last year a unique kitten came into my life. My heart belongs to all animals, but special needs animals hold a particular place. This is a result of my cat, Weaver, who was born without the use of her rear legs and was incontinent due to the nerve damage from various birth defects. Weaver was a part of my life for eight years until she passed due to kidney failure. She was the reason I rescued a special kitten from animal control when the plea came out over the rescue email lists of my area.

I was sitting at my desk trying to wade through the mountains of paperwork in front of me, when a plea for a six-week-old kitten, who had just been brought to an animal control in north Louisiana, came into my inbox. I found it odd that a plea for a kitten was going out on this list, as most people on the list were dog people, and emails about cats were rare. The subject line read: "Kitten with Deformed Legs at Animal Control: Needs Rescue," and the message was from a dog rescuer who happened to be in the animal control facility when the kitten was brought. She took photographs and quickly sent out the email.

The rescuer normally did not work with cats, but the little kitten pulled at her heart because the center was not going to even consider finding placement for her; the kitten was to be immediately euthanized. The lady convinced the officers to give her a day or two to try and find a rescue to take the kitten.

Upon seeing the pictures of the frightened kitten, I knew I had to do something. All I could think about was Weaver and how no one wanted to give her a chance when she was that age, yet she had become the light of my life. I quickly responded and spent the entire morning making phone calls and trying to convince the animal control director that I have experience with cats like this and can give the kitten a good life. I am glad that I did, as I later found out that no one else stepped up to help.

Two days later I met the kitten and a transport volunteer at a little convenience store. The kitten I received was in desperate need of a bath and lots of love. This was the same time that a plain and slightly unusual Scottish lady named

Susan Boyle had astonished the world with her powerful voice. Before she began singing during her first performance, everyone considered her a joke and judged her based on her appearance. When she opened her mouth, the beauty of her voice had people all over the world crying. I named the kitten Susan, as she seemed on the outside to be a total mess, but in her eyes I could see love and a fighter's spirit.

Susan was probably the result of someone trying to breed Cymrics, as she is a longhaired Manx (which is, by definition, a Cymric). Her rear legs were curled around like curly-Q fries. She could not urinate on her own and had to have her bladder expressed several times a day. I would come home during lunch every day to take care of her and give her a bath. She was a spunky kitten and was living up to her namesake.

Sue would go with me to adoption days on weekends, and everyone loved her. As she became older, she did not like the outings quite as much, so I would instead leave her home to play with the other cats, while I went to adoption days or to work.

I brought Sue to several veterinarians, who all said she was a wonderful cat who had a lot of spirit and determination. They agreed that when she was old enough, she should be fine to go under anesthesia to be spayed, but a turn of events soon had us all floored by the extent of her birth defects.

When she was a little over six months old, Sue developed a urinary blockage. I was unable to express her bladder one evening. Knowing that urinary blockages were deadly, I took her to the vet immediately. She was getting weak, and I was scared to death I would lose her, but I knew she was a fighter. I had to leave her at the veterinary clinic because they had no open appointments; I had basically just shown up and pleaded for help. After an hour or two, I received a phone call from her veterinarian.

"Hey, I've got an update for you." he stated.

"How's my little girl?"

"Well…that's the first thing we've got to talk about."

"What do you mean?" I asked very confused.

"Miss Susan is actually Mr. Susan."

"I'm sorry… There's nothing back there."

"Well he does have one thing… The rest is probably inside him, or he doesn't have them at all. He does present externally as if he is a female, but if you apply pressure back there, you will see he's a boy."

I was astonished. Susan had been to three different veterinarians, and nobody realized that he was male? Of course, I never went poking around back there to make sure, and nothing ever poked out when I had made him urinate, so I wasn't the wiser. We talked for a while to discuss the blockage. Apparently it is much more common for males to have urinary blockages than females. When a cat has a blockage, he or she must get to a veterinarian immediately, or death within a day or two is probable.

It was very lucky that I had to express Susan's bladder because I knew right away that he had a blockage. This is why it is so important to keep an eye on your cats to make sure they are using the litter box properly and not having any issues. Susan was lucky, and after three days at the veterinary clinic, he was now able to come home. I had to bring him back once more after about two days when he became blocked again, but after that he did very well. Thankfully he has not had another blockage since.

At that point I was facing a new dilemma...do I rename him? I was used to Sue being my little Susie-Q, so now what? My friend said that I should just keep the name Sue and say he was named after the Johnny Cash song, "A Boy Named Sue." I laughed and said that was a good idea. I think I jinxed myself at that point, as Sue has grown up to be quite the little tough guy. He is the most dominant cat in my house, feeling that he has to prove he is the biggest, baddest cat in our little world. This is funny since he is still relatively small with a female-looking face and long fur, which makes him look even more like a female cat. He's turning out to be My Boy Named Sue, and I love every minute of his antics.

Just think, a little over a year ago animal control would have euthanized this spunky fellow because they felt he couldn't live a normal life. It just goes to show that like in the case of Susan Boyle, we should not judge people or animals before getting to know them.

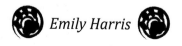 *Emily Harris*

Butter Me Up

I run to the kitchen, searching for the thud I had heard only moments before. "Oliver!" I say with exasperation. There, on the counter, sits the newest member of our family. He cocks his head to one side and blinks his beautiful, round blue eyes at me playfully. He answers me with a definitive "mier-r-r-ow" that sounds like a purred meow. His short, fluffy ivory coat glistens in the sunlight, and he begins washing his dark face with an equally dark paw.

From the other room I hear, "He went after the butter again, didn't he." It's more of a statement than a question.

I sigh, with a hint of a smile on my face. "Yes," I say.

On the floor lies the unfortunate stick of butter, still wrapped and full of little teeth marks, and I notice a large chunk is missing from one side. My husband adds helpfully, "Maybe we should use the butter dish next time."

I first met Oliver just four months ago, when I had flown to Denver, Colorado, to adopt him from Rocky Mountain Siamese Rescue. It was there that our adventure began.

It all started last summer, when I was looking for a cat to adopt in honor of our Snowshoe Siamese, Teddy, who had recently passed away. I had chosen to look for a cat from the same rescue that had saved an extremely thin and older Teddy and given him another chance. Browsing their website last summer, it wasn't long before I came across the captivating story of a very special cat. His name was Timber CO0343, and he was about 3½ years old. He had been found trapped in the window well of a foreclosed home. No one knows exactly how long he was there, but it was long enough for him to lose a lot of weight. He was only 4.6 pounds with brittle, broken whiskers and a dark, dull coat. I loved him right then and there.

After many conversations with his foster mom, I flew to Denver to officially adopt him. There, I met him in person for the first time, and I couldn't get over how handsome he'd become. A new, healthy coat had grown in with the wonderful care he'd received, and his whiskers had almost grown back, too. The only thing that hadn't changed about his appearance were those beautiful, big blue eyes.

As I held him for our adoption photo, I was instantly smitten. His fur was so soft beneath my fingertips. I wondered what he must think of me and of the unpredictable changes the course of his life was taking. Then he had gas, and I hoped that wasn't my silent answer, as I mentally calculated the hours until we'd be back home.

Fortunately, our trip home and subsequent integration went by quietly and quickly. We dubbed him Oliver after the Dickens character of the same name. He slowly got to know our other two cats and seemed comfortable for the most part. He was very quiet and didn't have much of a purr. I had to put my ear to his side to hear it, and it usually only lasted a few seconds. He wasn't a lap cat, and although he'd let us hold him, I wasn't sure how close he really wanted to be to us. He seemed to love our attention and loved to play even more, but I could tell he was still trying to figure out what his special place in our family was. I just wanted to know that he was happy.

One evening he followed us into the family room like usual. He sat by the edge of the room, and as I looked at him, it dawned on me that he was waiting for his invitation. His foster mom had noticed this about him, but the meaning hadn't really clicked with me until now. With him not being a lap cat, I hadn't known how close he wanted to be to us, and I didn't want to push him. I was used to living with demanding lap cats, so this was a new thing for me.

I grabbed a soft fleece blanket and spread it out next to me on the couch. I gave it three quick pats when I was finished and then called his name. Oliver gave this lovely, trilling meow to answer me and came running over, obviously thrilled that I had finally caught on. He immediately started bathing himself and settled in for a long nap right next to me. I sat there and petted him for a long time; I was thrilled.

That night I tried the same thing when I went to bed, but Oliver was off playing with the other cats. He had definitely found his place with them and enjoyed sneaking up on his older cat brother, Bastian. I settled into bed and was almost asleep, when I felt movement and something pressing against my back. I then heard the familiar sounds of licking. It was Oliver, and he was home.

Today Oliver enjoys following us around the house or napping in his favorite spots, which are usually near us or near the other cats. He's become quite the conversationalist, always with the most melodic meow. I think of it as his version of a purr. And when I see those beautiful, round eyes staring back at me from the countertop and throw away yet another piece of food that's been decorated with kitty tooth marks, I know he's happy, and I just have to smile.

And remember to use a butter dish.

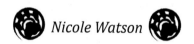 *Nicole Watson*

Rich Rewards

Volunteers who rescue domestic animals are never surprised by the depths of human cruelty toward innocent pets. They are also not surprised by the grace and forgiveness demonstrated by abused pets after the trauma they have suffered.

A good example of this is a small black cat I recently helped rescue in East Ocean View, VA. In June I spotted this cat, nicknamed Fiona, scrounging for food near an apartment building. What made her remarkable was her tail—about six inches of hairless, bloody skin and bone. I was told by a lady in the adjacent buildings that the cat had been dumped by a family that moved away. Some teens in the area had caught her and placed a rubber band around her tail. Unfortunately, the chances of finding the culprits in that 19th Bay neighborhood were pretty slim.

Fiona, abandoned, starving, and now in intense pain, was understandably wary of people. It took me more than six weeks to finally trap her and get her to a vet, where her tail was amputated to a tiny stump. Before the surgery, Fiona's tail was badly abscessed and crawling with maggots. Fiona was spayed and vaccinated, thanks to Cat Rescue, Inc. The big question was whether or not she would ever be social enough to be a pet after all she had been through.

As soon as Fiona arrived at the Cat Rescue foster's home, it was obvious she was truly the ogre who became a princess. As much pain as she must have suffered, she bears no grudges and is sweet and loving, softly meowing and eager to be petted. Fiona has healed and discovered the joys of plentiful food, toy mice, and fellow felines, which has prepared her to be a family pet.

It turns out that in addition to her own plight, poor Fiona was caring for three kittens. After Fiona was trapped, the eight-week-old black kittens gathered around her. They scattered quickly, but I was later able to trap them all, and they are now with a foster. The tiniest female kitten's tail was also damaged, which will require surgery. Gentle hands will tame them, and they, too, will be placed up for adoption.

As much as I detest those who abuse animals, I am in awe of creatures like Fiona, who survive abuse and are still able to trust and love. It also makes the effort to rescue and aid these animals one of the most rewarding experiences in my life.

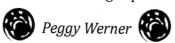 *Peggy Werner*

Kitty Kwips

Merci BeauCoo: I was visiting my parents when a stray cat caught my eye. She was a little orange cat, barely more than a kitten, lurking at the edge of their back yard for days. Cats weren't allowed in my parents' house because they were both allergic, so I took to hanging out in the back yard to feed and pet her. She had the strangest little purr that sounded exactly like a pigeon cooing! One day I was upset and brooding in my room, when my mom came in and deposited the cat on my lap, saying she thought I needed some "cat therapy." Pigeon cheered me right up, and at that moment I decided there was no way she was going back outside. These days when Pigeon curls up with me, she coos so loudly you'd think I had a whole room full of pigeons! -*Andrea Westerfeld*

Feral Friends: My friend Joe trapped a feral cat and had her updated on shots, tested for disease, and spayed before returning her back to her habitat. Upon finding out she had feline leukemia and that the other cats were picking on her, I decided to take her in. Even though I'm asthmatic, I laid with her, petted her, and told her she would be okay. That was over a decade ago, and Maya has been doing fine, even though the vet said she'd only live a year or two. We've since adopted Jody-Jean, who someone dumped out of a car. Maya mothered her until Jody-Jean was okay. What have I learned? Ferals make great pets, too. -*Monica Affleck*

Fall Flame

The name Akio means "Autumn Boy" in Japanese. I have visited Japan several times and thus wanted to give my kitty a Japanese name. But my Akio has another name: The Flying Mush. This is because when I call his name, he jumps into my arms, purrs, makes sweet mushies with his paws on my shoulder, and sometimes licks my face. Later on, he sits on my chest while I watch TV. He is a big flame-point Meezer boy, so the only reason why he isn't a lap cat is because he just doesn't fit on my lap. His companion, elderly Chantee, sits next to me by my side, and all is peaceful.

How did I acquire Akio? I adopted him from Virginia Siamese Cat Rescue on October 3 of last year; this is his official "gotcha day." Just two months earlier, I had lost my 12-year-old Oriental Longhair cat, Arian, to acute kidney failure; she was being treated for diabetes and her kidneys suddenly crashed. Sadly, she had to be put to sleep. My other cat, 14-year-old Chantee, a tortie lynx point Siamese, was inconsolable, roaming around my apartment and yowling at the loss of her friend. I knew that I had to get her another companion—not to replace Arian, as no cat can be replaced—but to take a unique place in my home as Chantee's companion.

I have always loved Siamese cats, and up until around 20 years ago, I had been breeding and showing Siamese. However, for various reasons I gave up breeding but continued to keep Siamese and related-breed cats as spayed/neutered pets.

About four years ago, I ran across the organization Siamese Cat Rescue Center (SCRC) through my employer's Combined Federal Campaign donation program. I designated a portion of my CFC donation to SCRC and they began sending me Meezer Meows, their entertaining newsletter. I determined that, when I was going to acquire another kitty, I would adopt from SCRC. However, I had some elderly cats who were still perfectly healthy and happy.

Gradually, as the years went by, these cats succumbed to old-age diseases, and I was down to just Chantee and Arian. Once Arian went over the Rainbow Bridge and Chantee went into mourning, I contacted SCRC and applied for adoption approval. During the approval process, I had an interview with one of SCRC's adoption interviewers for matchmaking purposes. We decided that a young adult male Siamese would be best as a new companion for Chantee. I have always loved flame point Siamese and wanted this new kitty to be a flame point. I was told that flame point boys are usually very loving, cuddly, and affectionate.

Once approved, I went through the list of available flame point Siamese boys on SCRC's amazing website. Once I spotted a likely flame boy ready for adoption, I would contact the foster "meowmy" or "paw" who was caring for the kitty. Because flame point boys are usually very easygoing, most of them are popular and have many inquirers lined up to adopt them. This is what happened to me; I would spot a flame point, and when I inquired, I would discover that I was number two or number three in line. Usually someone in front of me would end up adopting the prospective cat. Then I saw the picture of a kitty with a broad flame face, mild blue eyes, and a description that stated he had just been swept away from a shelter to his foster meowmy's home and was unsure of the new situation; however, he had surprised his foster meowmy by purring and making biscuits with his paws. His name was named Stills, one of a trio of flame boys rescued together: Crosby, Stills, and Nash. I wondered, if he was shy with "issues," did I want to take a chance on him?

Twelve years earlier I had adopted Chantee, who had been very scared. It had taken me a few months to get her socialized, but now she is a calm, friendly kitty. So I inquired about this flame boy, and as it turned out, I was number one—the only one—on his list.

I asked about his story and was told that he, along with Crosby and Nash, had been rescued from a hoarder, a person with a mental illness that had felt driven to collect and keep 40 cats. He had arrived at a local shelter covered with fleas, trembling, and shy. I doubt that he would have been considered very "adoptable," cringing in the corner of the crowded shelter. Fortunately, the shelter had a relationship with SCRC, and he was taken to his foster home in the SCRC program, which probably saved his life. His foster meowmy reported that though he was frightened in new situations, he did respond to stroking. Slowly he began trusting more and even seeking affection. Still, I wondered, am I getting a cat with problems?

His foster meowmy and I chatted for a while, and I decided to take the plunge, pledging to adopt him. We made arrangements for me to drive from Maryland to Pennsylvania to pick him up. Because he was the color of autumn leaves, and I was adopting him in the autumn season, I would rename him Akio.

When I arrived at Akio's foster home, I met some very friendly Siamese kitties all looking for homes. I wondered if perhaps I should have considered one of them instead—especially when Foster Meowmy brought Akio down from upstairs, and he began trembling in fright upon seeing me. I thought to myself, "What in the world have I gotten into?" But I had given my pledge to this kitty, who had come from such a wretched existence.

Foster Meowmy loaded a struggling Akio into the carrier, and we began our drive home. While on the drive, Akio started panting with stress. Again, I thought, "What have I done? What issues am I going to have to deal with?"

Once we arrived home, after I put Chantee into a separate room, Akio promptly hid while I wondered what to do. Fortunately in his take-home kit, Akio's foster meowmy had thoughtfully included a feather wand toy. I started waving the feather toy, and Akio began tentatively inching out. We were started on the road to our acquaintance.

During the next couple of weeks, I realized that Akio, having lived with a hoarder and most likely been confined to a cage or carrier, was quite unused to the "vast" space of a one-bedroom apartment. I had to gradually teach him how to orient himself in such a free space. Akio had to learn a few more things, such as how to sit on a lap, but he was quite eager for these lessons. It really didn't take long for Akio to fulfill his destiny as a certified mush-kitty.

Right now Akio is very needy, craving affection and attention. I can understand why, as he was so deprived of these elements during the time he lived in that tragic hoarding situation. He spends some time dashing around the apartment, having the kittenhood he never had before. He still hates being loaded into a carrier to go to the vet for checkups. (Recently he had to endure the crate to have his teeth cleaned, and now they are shiny and white). I pledged to Akio that he would never have to live in wretched conditions, confined to a small cage or carrier, ever again. He and Chantee now sleep together; she no longer mourns for her lost companion. When Akio gets a bit rambunctious, Chantee gives him a swipe with her paw, never really hurting him, just teaching him respect for the elderly.

Akio is spoiled every day, and he deserves it. I no longer wonder about him or any issues. I know that I adopted just the right kitty for me.

 *Nina Boal*

MiniKitty Gets Rescued... Twice

MiniKitty was abandoned by our neighbors when they moved. I've never understood how anyone could do that; I wouldn't have been able to look at myself in the mirror. Our cat at the time (now deceased), Tigger, started palling around with MiniKitty, which is how I found him. If you know cats, you know that this is practically unheard of. He was probably not even one year old at the time, but the two became inseparable. We took MiniKitty in, and over the years he flourished.

MiniKitty has always been a very independent, tough-guy tomcat. I'd go on business trips for two weeks at a time and let him come and go from the house through his kitty door. The sitter would come and feed him, and he was always fine. Then, when he was about 12 years old, I came home from being out of town and saw that MiniKitty hadn't eaten any of his food for at least three days. Needless to say, I was worried sick. I had a feeling of dread in the back of my mind, like I'd never see him again. I didn't know what to do. I started making up "lost cat" posters and looking for him online. He wasn't wearing a collar and didn't have a microchip. What hope was there for finding a little lost kitty who was out in the big, scary world?

My friend Paul, who worked near an animal control office about a half hour away, said he'd look there for MiniKitty. I wasn't holding much hope for finding him so far away, but I was happy that Paul was at least giving it a shot.

Paul called me back and said they had a tabby, but he wasn't sure it was my boy. I texted him some photos while dreading the thought of him coming over with a cat who wasn't MiniKitty. Then what would I do?

But Paul called back and said that indeed this cat had been picked up on my street. By that time MiniKitty was so despondent that he didn't even recognize Paul, who had cat-sat for him on many occasions.

Paul brought MiniKitty home in a carrier box. I was so happy to see him; it was like getting a child back from a kidnapper. Paul said that as soon as they turned onto my street, MiniKitty started meowing, even though he was closed up in the carrier. But my poor kitty clearly had a case of post-traumatic stress disorder. He ate a little and then sat and drank his spring water for about a half an hour. Then he hobbled out to his room and curled up in a fetal position on the couch. Paul said he was with about 15 other cats, up on a shelf as far away from the others as possible. He also had infected bites on three of his paws and had lost four pounds, so he probably hadn't been eating or drinking at all.

Paul gave me a form from animal control that said our neighbor had caught him in a trap and turned him in. I could not believe that anyone could be so horrible to turn in my beloved kitty, who wasn't hurting anyone and had been in the neighborhood longer than the woman who trapped him. I couldn't really say much about it, though, because there is a leash law in my town.

MiniKitty had been one day away from being put to sleep. (They have room to keep them for only five days.) That really terrified me.

$300 in vet bills and $100 in animal control fees later, MiniKitty was well on his way to recovery. He's microchipped now, and when I'm not home, I leave him in the house, which he doesn't like one bit. When he's out, he definitely stays closer to home. The experience changed him, ironically making him much sweeter and more appreciative than ever before, and I've learned to not let my precious kitty out of the house unsupervised. Every day I have with him seems like kind of a miracle now.

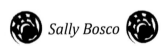 *Sally Bosco*

FIV+ and Positively Wonderful

One February I looked out the front door peephole to find a cat outside. When I opened the door, he had vanished like a shadow, so that's what we called him. This happened a couple of times. It turned out he had been staying under our front stoop in a snowstorm. When I realized this, I put some food out, and as he ate, I watched him through the peephole. I continued putting out a plate of food for him at 9 p.m. every night for six months, and he only failed to come by for his food once. The reason I fed him at 9 p.m. was because we had trained our cats to spend the night in the house. This was when there was a raccoon rabies scare, and we didn't want our cats to get into any trouble, even though they had all been vaccinated for rabies. We also didn't want our cats fighting with Shadow, so we fed him when they were inside.

Somehow Shadow and I became friends. I sat with him when he ate, and after dinner he would try to insert his foot through the front door. But I couldn't bring him inside because of all our other cats.

In early September, the weather was starting to get chilly again, so I put a cat carrier outside and fed Shadow in the carrier. When he went in, I closed the door and brought him inside. I put the carrier in a room and shut the door. In the morning, as had been previously arranged, I brought him to our vet to be tested for leukemia, FIV, and to be neutered. The vet called and said Shadow was about four years old and had tested positive for FIV. As was the thinking at that time, the vet told me I should do the responsible thing and put Shadow to sleep, but I told the vet I would instead give Shadow to a rescue group that had an FIV+ section.

Then I decided I hadn't made friends with Shadow just so he could spend his life in a cage. I called the vet back and asked to have Shadow neutered, which he did. When I retrieved Shadow from the vet, the technicians had been carrying him around and had found him to be a nice, friendly cat. I brought him home and put him in that same room. My husband, Gene, made an outdoor cage-type thing for Shadow, but Shadow didn't like it, so he became a house cat.

Shadow developed a urinary tract blockage from crystals in his urine. I read a book, and as it instructed, I started putting 1/16 tsp. of vitamin C crystals in each of his two daily meals. I only fed him canned food, didn't feed him fish, and put some ground psyllium husk in his food. He had a couple of blockage episodes, and the vet talked about doing some type of operation, but after Shadow had taken the vitamin C for a while, he never had any more blockages.

When we moved to a larger house, Shadow lived in my office, which was a much larger room than he had lived in at our previous house. I felt bad keeping Shadow isolated from his own kind, so I slowly introduced him to the other cats, at first only letting him be with them while we watched TV and supervised. Eventually he became one of them.

After our cat Gilley died, Shadow took over as a kind of gentle bully. He was friends with Ali and Buddy, but one night Shadow had a fight with Buddy and drew blood. I was afraid Buddy would get FIV. Shadow had been tested several times, and he always tested positive. Still, when I then had Buddy tested, I learned that Shadow had not transmitted the FIV to Buddy. Eventually I read somewhere that FIV+ cats can live almost normal lives with other cats and not transmit the virus unless there is a very serious fight.

According to my husband, Shadow always looked at me with love and devotion in his eyes. He would follow me around the house. Outside we had a cat fence system, which consisted of netting around the top of the fence. In the fall, leaves would get stuck in the netting. Since our cats didn't go out very much anymore, I untied the netting and let it hang down. One day I let Shadow out into the yard. I was not paying attention and suddenly noticed that Shadow wasn't there. I quickly looked under bushes and behind trees and couldn't find him. I started to panic. I called his name, and to my surprise, he climbed over the six-foot fence and came back into the yard. I took his speedy return to mean he had no wish to leave us.

During the last two or three years of his life, Shadow had gingivitis, a common condition in FIV+ cats. For some unknown reason, the vet didn't recommend pulling Shadow's teeth; he said it wouldn't help. So I did everything I could to make Shadow comfortable, even pureeing his food and bringing him to a vet who specializes in homeopathy.

Despite his condition, Shadow still seemed to want to live. He eventually developed hyperthyroidism, but I had the holistic vet treat him because I didn't want to hurt his mouth by giving him pills. His homeopathic medicines could be liquefied in a teaspoon of milk, and Shadow didn't object to taking them.

One summer morning Shadow wasn't doing well. He was staggering around. I called the vet and was going to bring Shadow to be put to sleep. Because the vet had a plane to catch for his vacation, he wasn't able to come to the house, which he usually did in these situations. He would meet me at his office. Just before heading out, I left Shadow alone in a room for a couple of minutes. When I returned, he had died. Perhaps he wanted to die in privacy.

Shadow was our wonderful cat for 11 years, and if he really was about four when we took him in, he lived to be a normal age for a cat. We enjoyed the time we had with him.

 *Sarah Qualman*

Baffling Brotherhood

After the passing of our beloved 16-year-old cat, Kringle, my husband, Tim, and I almost immediately became the proud parents of two affectionate and rambunctious four-month-old kittens, Jed and Jackson. Do not pass go. Do not collect $200. No free parking. In fact, let's donate $200 to the shelter, and as we take our new kids to the car, let's admire our lovely parting gift: a parking ticket plastered to the windshield in the rain. No worries. Nothing could dampen the spirits of our baby parade. We had just won the kitten lottery.

Brothers from the same mother, our kittens have different fathers. While I never knew it was possible, the scientific term for this is *superfetation*. As it turns out, roughly 10% of female cats go into heat between the third and sixth week of pregnancy, and although these cycles are rarely fertile, it is possible for a cat to carry fetuses of different ages that resulted from separate matings.

Typically the youngest litter is delivered prematurely with the oldest and is therefore unable to survive. In extremely rare cases, the youngest kittens remain in-utero until fully developed. So I guess we have ourselves some rare and miraculous little super-beasties. Against scientific odds, these guys found a way to be together, and that's how they'll remain.

Satisfying my biological need to mother and nest, my new family and I have already accomplished a great deal together: dog introductions, two wellness visits, two dewormings, survival of four respiratory infections (my husband and myself included), 28 days of Bartonella (a bacterial infection especially prevalent in shelter kittens, a.k.a. cat scratch fever) treatment (x2), growth spurts of up to a pound a week, trying out several sporty scratching posts, adjusting to wearing collars (the cats, not us), scheduling two neuters (again, the cats), and offering a sundry of toys. Wait, this was just in four weeks?

"Welcome to fresh new parenthood!" I said to myself, as the little lives of my purring boys rested literally in my hands. Having had cat companions for over 30 years—since I was six—I thought I had this gig down. As it turns out, I knew nothing-zilch-nada-zero about kittens. But you can bet, after a month of full immersion, I do now.

Here's what I've learned:

- Kittens can carry diseases and still look cute. Very. Cute.

- Kittens require high-calorie food and transition to low-calorie food at five or six months. No, they will not tell you this. They'll just pork out and curl up in a food coma.

- Kittens sleep a lot.

- Kittens wake up energized *a lot*.

- Kittens lose their teeth, sometimes in each other's head. When kittens are teething, they chew furniture legs, picture frames, watering cans, and toes. To spare household items and personal appendages, we've introduced "Tadah!" straws. (We take out a straw and say "Tadah," while twirling it for the kittens. They love it!)

- Kittens get into, onto, and under everything. We're bolting furniture to the walls.

While these practical aspects are good to know, here's another really important thing: When kittens do something amusing, sweet, or downright funny, it's best to grab your camera right then and there. Kittens take on new projects by the minute, outgrowing or rarely repeating photo-worthy moments. Breaking their mother's heart, kittens grow from babies to teenagers in less than 60 seconds, or so it seems.

Things I thought I knew about cats are unraveling daily. The kittens do everything that my older cat never did, even when he was four months old. Our older cat preferred the floor to heights. The kittens prefer to sit on your head, while you're standing, and they'll climb whatever it takes to get up there. Although he was clearly the alpha in this household, our older cat never harassed the dogs. The kittens swat at dog faces, tails, and feet. They walk under dog bellies, over dog backs, and fly across our Newfoundland as he naps to attack looming shadows of dust elephants lurking on the other side. Our older cat never ate house plants. The kittens, on the other hand, constantly graze from my "salad bar," playing in the dirt and toppling pots for amusement. We're still morphing, learning, and growing together. It's been nothing less than fun and funny.

Cheers to our very happy rescued family, the kittens from homelessness and us from the loss of a best cat friend, and cheers to a long, healthy, and hysterical life—together. We wouldn't have it any other way.

 *Kim Clune*

Kitty Kwips

Meezer Express: Hours before a forecasted ice storm, two courageous rescuers intervened with a breeder-gone-bad situation and removed more than a dozen cats from bare outdoor kennels, where they would surely have died from exposure. Some were already ill and did not survive. Damian was one of the lucky ones who recovered at one volunteer's home until he could be welcomed into ours. Damian's other rescued siblings and cousins have found homes all over the country. Four of them traveled from Texas to Oregon via Meezer Express, a volunteer Siamese-cat transport organization, where they are now enjoying the life to which they might not have become accustomed, had it not been for the wonderful, caring members of Austin Siamese Rescue. As for Damian, he is completely spoiled and enjoys his life with our other cats, especially his best friend Wally. He is much too fine a cat for plain folk like us, but he loves us anyway, and we him!
-*Crystal Wood*

Cure for Cancer Blues: I had breast cancer 3½ years ago, and while I was going through chemo, I had a few really bad days. My cats sensed that I was feeling terrible, and while I was lying on the couch after my chemo treatment, they both jumped on the couch with me: one lay on my chest and the other cuddled next to me. I petted them both for a little while and immediately started feeling better. I love my girls and would not trade them for anything. They helped me through a bad time in my life. Thank you Cookie and Sophie, you're a great example of how wonderful pets can be. -*Yvonne Chapek*

Souls Intertwined

I knew it was going to happen.

His name was Mr. Wink. He was my black-and-white cat of an unknown species, with long legs and flipping tale. His Roman nose, complete with little bump, had a small black square under it that could have been interpreted as a "Hitler" mustache, but that was much too bleak of a reference for a cat as sweet as Mr. Wink.

There was a song from the Jimmy Durante show that I used to sing to him, which became "our song." Jimmy, a famous old Vaudevillian comedian who also had a big nose, used to sing, "Wink-a-dink-a-dooooo, a dink-adoooo, adinkadooo," while he side-stepped and shook the crumpled fedora hat he always wore in one hand. I often cooed that song to Mr. Wink. He seemed to like it a lot.

Wink was of an unknown age, as he was a skinny, sad neighborhood stray when we moved into this house. He quickly became a guardian to my five-pound calico cat called Baby. He was her protector and lover. She was 21 years old. Baby had been an outdoor cat for years, also a stray, found at about eight months behind a washing machine. Being as little as she was, she was "low cat on the food chain" and somehow knew the tiny spaces in which to crawl when danger was around.

When she and Wink met, I was afraid he would try and drive her off. Much to my astonishment, Baby did the hissing and Mr. Wink did the cowering, until one day I noticed that the hissing had stopped, and they were eating out of the same bowl. Soon Wink was grooming Baby, biting her, and meowing to her, with his tail flipping wildly as he would wind himself around her in the little donut bed they now shared. She allowed him completely into her life, and I allowed him completely into mine. The name Mr. Wink came from the fact that his left eye was smaller than his right, thus he always looked like he was winking at us. He and Baby were inseparable. Wherever she went, he went. The only time either of them would come inside was for breakfast in the mornings. I would leave the door open, and they would march in and out, in and out, as cats are want to do, with anticipation.

Their blissful partnership lasted into the 7th year. One morning I came out to greet the happy couple and get their bowls for their morning "fancy feast." The donut bed was empty. This was very unusual.

As I walked around the side of the house, to my horror, I saw smears of blood and then one last large drop of blood, followed by nothing. It was as if whomever had been taken away had vanished into thin air.

Was it Wink or Baby?

After about 20 minutes, it was Mr. Wink who rounded the corner of the garden. He was walking very slowly. I knew then it was Baby who had been taken away. In her old age she seemed to have lost most of her hearing. I imagined that whatever had come, Wink had sensed it and run away, and by the time her little five-pound self reacted, it was too late.

What really happened, I may never know. There is speculation it could have been a red tail hawk, which definitely would explain her disappearance "into thin air." They are around my home—big, beautiful and aggressive—fully capable of grabbing a five-pound deaf cat. Whatever it was, I hoped it happened quickly. The notion that little Baby suffered in any way was unbearable.

Wink never recovered. It seemed he had lost his reason for being. He wandered aimlessly. He came in the house more and more. Wink had been Baby's caregiver. Now I was his. He redefined the expression by the way he took care of Baby. His life was defined by her existence. Now that she was gone, he seemed unsure of what to do. He disappeared for hours at a time and never again slept in their donut bed. He became disinterested in food. He seemed slower and needier. I encouraged him inside more, stroked him more, and loved him more.

I don't know when I noticed that his scent had changed. He had a somewhat acrid, salty scent instead of the outdoors scent that often blew in with him when he came indoors. And the color of his nose went from pink to almost white. He was dropping weight rapidly; I could feel every rib. But it was the notches on his spine and the caved-in wells on either side of it above his haunches that really caught my attention. The vet diagnosed him with abdominal cancer. I just remember how robust he was in April, and here it was only November, and he had become a shadow of himself, although sweeter than ever and more dedicated to my presence.

The vet said it was just a matter of time. He advised me to take him home.

With new awareness of how finite our relationship had become, I began cooking turkey burgers, fresh tuna, and fresh chicken for Wink. He even seemed to enjoy kitten kibble. My vet suggested I let him go out during the day but bring him in at night, as he had no meat on his bones to keep him warm and no energy to defend himself from anything. The days fortunately were warm and sunny, and at twilight I would bring him in. Wink quickly learned his way to my bedroom upstairs, and when he seemed to be missing one afternoon, I found him on my bed purring away. He took to sleeping there each night, often purring himself and me to sleep.

He would wake at dawn, eager to go outside. He would disappear for several hours. I often saw him perched on the wall or sitting in the middle of nowhere, staring into space. It seemed he was communing with something I knew little or nothing about.

Wink grew thinner and weaker, but he did not appear to be in any pain. I constantly talked to him, and he looked at me so thoughtfully it was as if he understood my sentiment.

On this last day, I picked him up from his outdoor perch at about 3:30 p.m. and brought him in. He immediately began to purr and "make muffins" before stretching out and falling right to sleep.

I went out for the evening, and when I came home, Wink was still on the comforter in my office. I decided to let him stay there instead of taking him upstairs to my bed. I grabbed a pillow and a quilt and lay down next to him.

It was about 4:45 a.m., when I heard a thud. I realized Wink had either tried to get off the couch or had fallen. I tried to grab him, and he made the first cry of distress I had ever heard him make. I took him in my arms. The scent I had smelled before was stronger, and it seemed to come from some kind of secretion coming out of his nose.

He was having trouble breathing. I knew the end was happening. I tried to comfort him by holding him, so he knew I was there. He gasped a couple of times before his front legs stiffened and spasmed, relaxed, and then spasmed again.

Suddenly, the strangest thing happened. My whole body began to vibrate. I could actually hear the sound. It was almost as if I were purring. I became dizzy and clammy and felt like I was going to faint or throw up. I felt afraid and knew something profound was happening. It was as if some unfamiliar energy had made its way into my body. As I try and describe it, it felt as if I had more inside of me than I could contain...and during that moment, I knew I had two souls inside of me.

Wink's front legs stiffened one more time and then his head fell limp. I knew he was dead. In my arms. I lay him softly on the comforter and waited for the light. He still looked alive to me. Just asleep. I was sure I could still hear and feel him purring. I stroked him and stroked him, continuing to talk to him for almost an hour and a half.

The sun began to rise. It was Thanksgiving morning. I had once started to dig a little grave for Baby at the edge of some young wild native oaks in my yard. Now it was Wink's. That seemed fitting. I hoped it was big enough for him.

I left him lying peacefully on the comforter and went down to the hole. I cleared away the ivy and made it a little deeper. Then I went back to get Wink. What would it be like to lift him? Would he flop over? Would he break? I had no idea. Very gently I lifted him. I was shocked. He felt like a feather. But he also looked exactly the same. Except for his eyes. They were gone. Just hollows remained. I knew it was because his soul had left.

I had put down a bed of ivy leaves at the bottom of the grave, and Mr. Wink fit in perfectly. I covered his small head and ears with more ivy leaves and then put handfuls of dirt over his body. I was worried I wouldn't have enough dirt to fill the hole, but I did. And that was it.

I believe Wink died partly of cancer and mostly of bereavement. I don't believe he ever got over the loss of Baby. But the love and bond we found in each other was truly indescribable. He knew how much I understood and loved him, and his love for me is undeniable. I will never forget that strange mingling of our souls. He taught me something so profound. I will always remember it and hold it close. Rest in Peace, my dearest Mr. Wink...a-dink-a doooo.

 *Lin Shaye*

Kitty Gets a Name

Kitty huddled by the icy dumpster wall. The piercing cold felt like needles sticking into his skin. Kitty's tummy cramped from pangs of hunger.

Mother Cat warned, "Run when you see people. You never know if they are mean or kind. Stay away from dogs and coyotes because they will bite you. Every time you hear the big garbage truck approach, you must run to the alley."

Kitty asked his mother, "Why do you call us all Kitty? We're each different."

Mother Cat replied, "You're all my kittens."

One morning Kitty saw a woman approach the dumpster. He cowered in a dark corner along with his brothers and sisters. The woman held out her hand. Inside her palm was a piece of meat. The smell pulled Kitty to crawl closer. Two of his brothers followed close behind.

Kitty sat up, placing his front paws together.

"Look, you're praying!" The woman fed him the delicious morsels.

Kitty's 10 brothers and sisters circled frantically, meowing, "Feed me. Please, feed me!"

Kitty realized, "If I show off, I'll get fed first."

The woman came often. She gave Kitty food each time he prayed. The kitties weren't afraid of her anymore.

After one feeding, the woman picked up one of Kitty's sisters and placed her in a crate. "You're going to be adopted."

Kitty mewed as he watched the woman leave with his sister.

After that the kittens scattered whenever they first saw the woman. She would wait with food. The kittens were starving and hunger always won over caution.

One by one, the woman caught the kittens.

Mother Cat meowed every time she lost one of her children.

One snowy morning Kitty's stomach growled from hunger. He forgot to run away.

The woman grabbed Kitty while he gobbled the delicious food.

Kitty wiggled, but the lady held on tight.

"Good Kitty," she said as she put him in a crate.

Kitty howled, "I'm scared. Let me out of here!" Kitty threw himself against the bars of the crate but couldn't escape. Kitty mewed a sad, long cry.

"My name is Sharry," said the woman. "We're going to take a little drive in my car."

Kitty banged the bars until he hurt.

"Settle down, little one," said Sharry. "You're rocking the car back and forth! I know you are afraid, but it will be okay."

Sharry stopped the car and carried the crate into a building. She said, "We're finally home."

She unlatched the crate and placed morsels of food in front of Kitty.

Kitty trembled in the back corner. Was this a trap? He sniffed the air and the carpet. He scanned the large room. It was warm and quiet.

Kitty inched forward to the food until he heard a noise. He whirled around to see a huge dog trotting into the room. Kitty ran under a chair. He trembled.

A tall woman followed behind. She knelt. "Hi, little Kitty. I'm Jane and this is Sita. We won't hurt you."

Kitty inched out from his hiding place. The large dog's cold nose gently nudged Kitty, and Kitty hissed. Jane laughed and petted Sita's head.

"Kitty is afraid that he is going to be bitten," said Sharry. Sharry picked up Kitty and placed him on Jane's lap.

Kitty felt his heart thundering against his chest. "I'm going to pet you," Jane explained. "You are so beautiful. Your black fur is silky soft. I love that one little white spot on your chest." Jane stroked Kitty under his chin, behind his ears, and up his back.

"Oh, this is nice!" thought Kitty. "My mother licked me, but I've never felt like this before."

Next, Kitty watched Jane place a bowl of food on the floor. "This is more food than I've ever seen before." Kitty got on his hind feet and placed his paws together.

"He's praying!" Jane laughed. "I love this kitty. I'm going to adopt him."

Kitty gobbled the food for fear it would disappear. Then Jane bounced an orange ball on the floor. It jingled. It rolled. It rattled. Kitty thought, "This is more fun than playing with the cans in the dumpster."

Sita wagged her tail and nudged Kitty. Kitty could tell this was a friendly dog. Jane was friendly, too. He liked the food. He liked the toys. He even liked the dog.

Jane petted Kitty. "I need to give you a name. I'm going to call you Cesar."

"Cesar: a name of my own. I'm not just Kitty anymore."

Cesar's chest rumbled. He was startled. "What was that?"

"Listen to you purr," Jane smiled.

"I'm a happy cat." thought Cesar. "I have a name. I'm safe and warm. I'm no longer hungry. I have a family who loves me—I am home."

About The Story of Cesar: *This story of Cesar is true. One awful day some people in a restaurant watched someone throw a pregnant cat out the window of a car. That mother cat had 11 kittens, and they all lived.*

They were born in a dumpster. The people in the restaurant brought them scraps of food. Some rescue volunteers came, played with the kittens, and gave them food. Eventually the kittens were taken away and adopted.

Meanwhile, I had lost my beloved cat, Molly, two days after Christmas. I have a hearing ear dog named Sita. My friend Sharry was one of the rescuers, and she knew how much I missed Molly.

In February, when Cesar was nine months old, Sharry caught him and brought him to her house. She told me later that the kitten banged so hard in the cage the car actually rocked back and forth! She wasn't sure this experiment was going to work. Would I be ready for another kitten, and would the kitten be ready for an owner?

One day I went to Sharry's house for a visit. When Sita and I entered, Sharry placed the scrawny little kitten in my lap. The kitten accepted my touch. (He had never been in a lap before). He jumped down and stood on his hind legs, clapping his front paws together. The rescuers had called him "the praying kitten." He then exposed his belly in the vulnerable position and went over to rub noses with Sita.

The kitten received the name Cesar that day and came home with us. He is presently three years old, several pounds heavier, and has a name. Sharry never heard him purr either, but he purrs all the time now!

 *Jane Biehl*

Stings Like a Bee

I saw two tiny cats at the edge of the back yard, so I put some food out and stood by the back door, watching them eat. If I moved a muscle, they vanished. One weekend I was talking on the phone when my husband yelled, "Come, quick!" There was one of the cats hanging upside down, dangling by her back leg, which was caught in the six-foot stockade fence. We freed her, putting her into a pillowcase and the case into a cat carrier, and then we took her to the emergency vet. As she was getting fixed up, we went to the immediate care center in the front of the building for treatment of my husband's bitten and scratched arm. When we returned to the emergency vet, we were told there was nothing they could do for the young feral cat; rehab was out because she was too wild.

We brought her home and put her in a room in our house. She was only about six months old. She would cower and hiss any time anyone entered the room. It wasn't possible to get near her. We couldn't release her because she was now crippled and would be unlikely to survive on her own. I never saw her companion, whom we believed to be her mother, again.

We tried to bring her to the vet to be spayed by putting some acepromazine, a tranquilizer, into her food, but the vet found her to be anemic from flea infestation, so he was unable to spay her. She went into heat a couple of times.

Eventually we fumigated the room while she was at the vet's office, and we were finally able to get the fleas and anemia under control and have her spayed. Even if the flea repellents put between the shoulder blades had been available then, we would not have been able to get near enough to put it on her.

We named her Ali after the famous boxer Muhammad Ali, since she was a fighter. My husband put a screen door on her room, so she could get used to seeing the other cats. She really had no problems with cats, it was people she feared. But Ali gradually became tamer, and after three years, we let her outside for the first time. She went out and came in with the other cats, but we couldn't stand near the door, or she wouldn't go through it. She eventually became trusting enough to let us pet her, but we still couldn't pick her up.

Ali had a bad heart murmur, so giving her acepromazine in order to be able to put her in a cat carrier and transport her to the vet was risky. As Ali aged, she became increasingly afraid to go in and out through the doorway. We gave her the last ½ acepromazine tablet I had, so we could put her in a carrier and move to another house. There, in this much larger house, Ali became an indoor cat. We stopped giving her rabies shots or taking her to the vet. She got along well with our other cats and was especially friendly with Chance and Buddy, our black-and-white cats.

When she was almost 18, Ali developed hyperthyroidism. By then she had lost most of her teeth, which had decayed and been pulled by the vet. She became mellow enough to be picked up and put in a carrier for occasional vet visits.

The majority of our cats had either been taken from the streets or adopted from a shelter as adults, making their exact age somewhat uncertain. We had to rely on the vet's best guess. In Ali's case, we knew she was around six months old when we found her because she hadn't yet gone into heat. We know she was a member of our family for a month longer than 18 years. Although Ali had the least vet care of any of our cats, she lived to be older than all of them.

 *Raffaela Dwyer*

Blindsided Boys

I had three boy kitties for a long while, but I really wanted to adopt a girl. I'd previously fostered cats, so I knew I needed just the right girl to mix with my three boys. There had been a hopeful, but she only loved me, not the boys. With a broken heart, I sent her on to a better home situation.

Then a coworker mentioned she'd seen "my girl" online with a different rescue organization in Baltimore. Well, I knew it couldn't have been that cat, but I looked her up anyway. This sweet kitty, Solstice did resemble the kitty I had rehomed, with one huge difference: Solstice actually liked other cats! Plus, she was a former mama kitty, and she'd adopted some orphaned kittens and raised them, too. I was immediately smitten and wrote to ask about her.

It was kismet, and within two weeks, "my girl" Solstice came home to her three ornery "brothers." Sadly, she looked so much like her predecessor that the boys wanted nothing whatsoever to do with her. She remained in isolation, and the boys stood in the doorway and hissed to voice their displeasure. But it was still early days, barely a week since she had come to live with us. I was discouraged but not in despair.

Then, one morning as I was walking to the train station, I noticed a group of people surrounding an SUV parked alongside a busy Washington D.C. street. Crouched beneath it were two tiny fuzzballs. They'd been cornered, but no one knew quite what to do with them, so I reached down and scruffed them both. A longhaired tortoiseshell kitten and a Siamese-mix kitten, both tiny and about four-weeks-old, shivered in either hand.

DC Animal Control was called, and I waited with the kittens until they arrived. I went home to my lonesome Solstice and three ornery boys, still thinking about those two kittens. And then I called DC Animal Control...

A week later two tiny kittens came home "to be short-term fosters." Solstice fell in love with them immediately, and they adored her right back. With all the wild kitten antics going on in the foster room, the boys totally forgot they hated Solstice!

That was a year ago. They've all been here ever since. It's been wild, but it took two orphans from Washington to integrate my lovely, shy, sweet, and kind Baltimore street mama.

 *Karen Hammond*

Kitty Kwips

Serious Schedule: At a PETCO adoption event, I saw a very proud male Siamese cat sitting on his foster mother's lap and growling at everyone who walked by. I knew right away that he was trying to protect his foster mommy and actually wasn't mean. Underneath the table in a cat carrier, hidden under a blanket was a precious, terrified little girl. When I placed her on my lap, she began playing with the boy kitty's tail before washing herself and then taking a nap. They both came home with me that day. Ten years later, Bourque and Shani have my husband and I wrapped around their paws! They tell us when it is time to wake up, when the gas fireplace needs to be turned on, and when it's snack or massage time. In essence, they are pretty serious about their schedule, and we are very serious about what wonderful additions they have been to our family. -*Jeri Kay Lockwood*

Uncanny Urchin: The first time I saw Uni I was driving on the highway, when I noticed something on the side of the road. "Road kill, poor thing," I thought to myself. But then I realized she was moving! I looped back around to the spot where I had seen the cat, but she was gone. Two weeks later someone sent me an email: "I found a kitty on the freeway Thursday night; she was moving. I pulled over and picked her up... They are going to euthanize her tomorrow afternoon. Please help the kitty." I contacted the guy, and he confirmed it was an orange tabby. It was a miracle! As a vet tech, I was able to help her, especially with the generous assistance of those who sent donations to assist with her medical costs. Thanks to them she is now the healthiest and happiest kitty ever! -*Anonymous*

Where's the Tooth Fairy When You Need Her?

The house was just too empty after losing our 16-year-old Misty to renal failure, so my husband and I decided to visit our local animal shelter to see who was available. We walked into a room where there were approximately 15 cats lounging around and playing. The minute we stepped through the door, a black-and-white kitty walked right up to my husband and started rubbing against his legs while purring. I walked around and checked out other kitties, while my husband gave his attention to the tuxedo-type kitty wrapping himself around his leg. My husband was ready to take that kitty home with us that day, but I had my eyes on a calico female. We decided to wait another day and think about it.

We went back again the next day and the day after that. On each visit, the tuxedo kitty immediately came up to my husband to say hello, whereas the calico kitty walked proudly around with her head and tail held high, completely ignoring us. By the third day, I couldn't resist the little black-and-white guy, either. He certainly seemed friendly and kept telling us by his actions that he wanted us to take him home.

On the way home from the shelter that day with Mario in a carrier, we stopped at our veterinarian's office for a prearranged visit to have Mario checked over. We were told he had an upper respiratory infection, his teeth needed to be cleaned, and his gums were a little red. No problem, we thought. We can handle this.

We took Mario home, showed him where the litter box was in the basement, and let him explore from there. After a few minutes of following him around in the basement, my husband sat down in the recliner. Mario immediately jumped onto his lap and started purring. He didn't even care if he explored the remainder of the house; he just seemed to feel at home. In fact, when my husband and I got into bed that first night, Mario jumped right up onto the bed with us as if to say, "I know this is my bed, too." Mario seemed to know he had found his forever home and people.

By now you are probably picking up on the clues that Mario is one friendly lap cat. He's the official greeter when the doorbell rings, nearly tripping whomever is answering the door in the process. If we have guests over for the evening, he's right in the room with us, usually making himself at home on whichever lap he chooses. After all, he's sure everyone is going to love him, and they usually do.

Life was perfect for the three of us until we took him in to have his teeth cleaned. The vet cleaned the teeth and decided three of them needed to be pulled. This was the beginning of ongoing dental work that didn't end until Mario became toothless at the age of four. Infection continued to be a problem in Mario's gums, even though we tried various antibiotics. Finally, one day our veterinarian said, "I hate to tell you this, but I think Mario is one of those rare cats that is allergic to his own tooth decay." She recommended seeing an animal dentist in a city about 60 miles away. Yes, there is such a thing as a dentist for animals.

The dentist instructed us to take Mario's food away at midnight the night before his visit and to take away water in the morning. He explained that Mario would be given a series of deep X-rays, which have to be performed while the animal is sedated. After dropping Mario off, the dentist told us to go home and wait for his phone call letting us know what he had found. If any teeth had to be pulled, a decision could be made over the phone because Mario would still be sedated. We could pick Mario up at the end of the day.

To make a long story short, the dentist told us Mario had stomotitis, an inflammation of the mucous lining of the mouth structures. He pulled out all of Mario's remaining teeth that day, except for the four canines he hoped could be saved. We would have to do a good job of brushing those canines every day without fail.

We took Mario home that night after being supplied with a small toothbrush, chicken-flavored toothpaste for cats, and another round of antibiotics. The veterinary dentist gave us a thorough demonstration of how to properly brush a cat's teeth along with a very hefty bill. Poor Mario must have thought that bad man had stolen all his teeth while he was sleeping.

Infection continued to be a problem, and we had to give Mario more antibiotics, even though we were very faithful about brushing his teeth every day. When we returned to the dentist for his check up, the dentist decided that the four remaining canines would have to be pulled or Mario would continue to experience ongoing infection, which could possibly lead to other serious diseases or even death.

Thus, Mario's four remaining teeth were pulled, leaving him toothless at age four, after only living with us for 11 months.

We are not of wealthy means. In fact, we are both retired and living on a very limited income. Fortunately we had money in savings that we could draw from to pay Mario's vet bills. We now tease him and tell him he's our sweet, loveable, $10,000, non-pedigreed little boy, who may have to get a job to support us at some point.

We do not regret adopting this sweet boy. He has filled our home with life once again and given us a reason to get up, get moving, and keep going during the day, no matter how our bodies ache or hurt. He has fully repaid us by being very loveable, giving us reasons to laugh, cuddling with us when we feel sad, and expecting nothing in return except two people who love him and promise to give him a forever home. He even forgave us for taking him to the dentist.

There are no health guarantees when you bring an animal into your life, no matter if he or she comes from a shelter or a breeder. So why not take a chance on a rescued cat or dog? Most often they make wonderful pets. We are on our fourth rescued cat, and we don't regret any of them, including Mario, despite all his tooth problems. I wish you could meet our sweet boy in person; our toothless little guy would sell you on the idea of adopting a rescued animal within five minutes.

 *Mary Roever*

Shelter in a Storm

The fact that my nickname is Kat really doesn't have anything to do with the reason that I love cats. Actually, I love all animals, but cats are my favorite. My 16-year-old gray tabby, Tink, was rescued from a shelter a decade and a half ago. I scooped up my temperamental Siamese, Sixx, before he was taken to a shelter five years later.

Last year was very tough because I lost my job. One night last June I was cleaning out the litter boxes, and Tink and Sixx were just sitting there with looks of entitlement as they watched me scoop and bag, scoop and bag. I had just come in from mowing the lawn, which I didn't quite finish because of a thunderstorm. Overall it was just a crappy day, and I was stressed at the time. I said to the king and queen, "Tink, you are 16, and Sixx, you are 11. After you guys are gone, I swear to the good Lord above, I am no longer going to have any house cats. I will graduate to a small dog whom I can take with me."

Of course, because the good Lord has such a wonderful sense of humor, that moment brought a bright flash of lightening—the kind that includes a simultaneous deafening crack of thunder that could wake the dead! And then I heard the sweetest meow coming from outside the back screen door. I looked up and said, "Oh, you are really funny, Lord. Real. Funny."

I was actually expecting a very small kitten by the sound of her voice, but when I looked out, she was about eight-to-ten months at a guess. I opened the door, and she came wandering in like she knew the place. I have a linoleum floor in the kitchen, which she comfortably stretched across. By this time we had a whopper of a thunderstorm, and the new addition, Calli, followed me around like a puppy. She slept with me under the covers that night, as the other two looked on with disgust. You know exactly the look I mean.

The next day I had to go to work, so I put Calli out the back door with food and water and thought that if she was still there at noon, I would take her to the shelter to see if someone was looking for her. Since she was very nice and obviously not abused in any way, someone must have been missing her. I have to admit, on the way home at noon I was hoping that she was not there, as I don't like taking animals *to* the shelter—I prefer to take them *out*!

I walked through the front door very quietly and tiptoed to the back door window to peer through the blinds. There she was, looking up at me. I opened the door, and again she came in like she had always lived there. I had little time, but I had already called the shelter to warn them of my possible visit. I took Calli there and told them her story. I am a very animated person, so of course, I had to act it out. The good folks at the shelter already knew me by name and would not have expected anything less!

I left Callie there with specific instructions that if no one claimed her in five days I wanted her, but I had to be fair in case someone was looking for her. After work I felt bad that she was in the shelter, but I knew I had done the right thing. The neighborhood kids came over and asked if I had seen her. I thought maybe they knew where she had come from, but they had only been playing with her outside. The five days came and went. I was not getting a paycheck for a few more days, so the shelter kindly went ahead and spayed her and updated her on the necessary shots, agreeing to hang on to her for me until I got paid.

On June 25th, the day before I was to get Callie, Michael Jackson passed away. The news covered the TV stations for weeks. Being his age and having grown up with him and the Jackson family, I was devastated.

On June 26th I got paid and picked up Callie. I needed to pour my heart out to something or someone after Michael Jackson's passing, and Callie turned out to be the one. Then, one week to the day of Michael Jackson's passing, I lost my job of nine years. I lost another friend in between, and I found myself just treading water. I was single, 52 years old, and suddenly had no job, no insurance, and no security of any kind.

Today I am a fulltime student at National American University. Times are still hard, but I don't think I would have made it through losing my job *and* two very dear people in my heart if it were not for that sweet voice during the storm. I love my Calli-Co, who has many nicknames. My favorite is Mommy's Pretty Girl.

When I feel overwhelmed and I cry, Callie comes running from any room in the house, even if I try to be quiet. She comforts me and reminds me that I was there for her during the storm, and I will be rescued someday, too. Then all is well again. All four of us get along great, and I am glad for that storm. As humans we all feel lost and alone sometimes. I think of the stray cats and dogs who feel that way and don't even have shelter, and I'm glad I didn't leave Callie out in the storm. It's evident she was sent to me to comfort me during my "storm," which at the time I didn't even know was coming!

Lord, I will never be without cats. Thanks for knowing me better than I know myself.

 *Kat Talamantes*

Kindness of Strangers

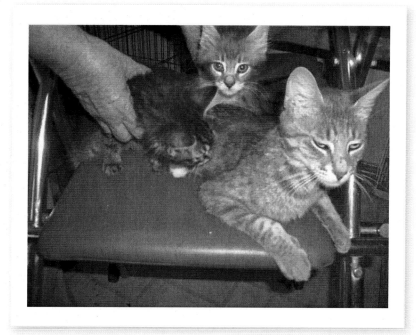

Hi, my name is Ashes. So far, my life has been a series of ups and downs. I was a loved pet for a time, but then I found myself pregnant and was dropped far from home. I was really frightened. Some boys shot me with BBs, and finding food was hard. But the wounds finally healed, and I learned to find enough food to keep myself alive.

Then I was taken into a new home and treated with love again. That's where my six handsome sons were born. I do not know why the family needed another pet, but suddenly there was this little dog in the house with us. I hissed at him and then found myself outside again with my three-day-old babies—at least this time we had a shed.

We received little food, so when the babies were about a month old, I decided to ask the lady next door for food. She gave me some! She even took me to a vet, where I got some shots. Then, a week later, when my babies started leaving the shed, I became concerned for their safety. I decided to take a chance on my new friend by placing them, one by one, in a large cardboard box in her carport. I guess she heard them because she took us all into her kitchen and placed my precious babies in a large crate.

This arrangement was great, and we stayed there for approximately five weeks. But the babies were getting larger, she had other pets, and she needed her kitchen for purposes other than housing my family. At that point, she took us to RescueCats, Inc. in Fayetteville, Georgia. At first I did not want to move again, but I have discovered it is a really great place. Living in a house with a lot of cats, I am learning to like other cats and even tolerate the dog. I am a loving cat, I really like people, I am great at purring, and I always try to crawl into the nearest lap. My sons have found good homes. They are great kittens, and I am so proud of them. I look forward to finding my own home soon, too.

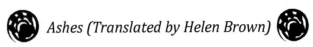 *Ashes (Translated by Helen Brown)*

Scotland Needs You

When the director of Texas Siamese Rescue asked if my husband and I would be willing to escort a cat to Scotland, we jumped at the chance! The adopter was Donna, a former New Yorker, who had met the Scotsman of her dreams and made a home and family with him in Scotland. They already had two Siamese cats, but Donna fondly remembered the "applehead" Siamese of her life in America; they are not popular in the UK, where the angular, "wedgy" type of cat is preferred. The lucky adoptee was Tommy Tinker (T.T.), a seal point applehead Siamese who had been fostered in Iowa but was spending his six-month quarantine at "Meezer Ranch" (Texas Siamese Rescue).

Our journey with T.T. began with an overnight flight from Houston to London Gatwick. We had a bit of a layover in London as we waited for our connecting flight to Edinburgh. T.T. had been cooped up in his carrier for many hours, so we let him out on his harness and leash, and wow, did he ever attract attention! T.T. is a big cat as far as Siamese go, and it was as if people had never seen anything like him. When they asked, I just told them that he came from Texas, where everything is bigger!

At last we arrived in Edinburgh and met Donna, her husband, and their two wonderful children. We drove to their house in the beautiful Perthshire countryside, and there T.T. found himself home at last. When he got out of the carrier in Donna's house, he sniffed around a bit and then stretched out on the carpet to relax, giving us a look that said, "Okay, I'm home now. Thanks for the lift!"

It was the trip of a lifetime for us, as after we left Donna's house we went to see London, Stonehenge, and other sites we never thought we would be able to see. When we tell people the "excuse" for our trip, they look at us as if we are completely crazy, and I wish I had a dollar for everyone who asked, "Why did you have to take a cat to Scotland? Don't they have cats there?" Of course they have cats in Scotland—but they didn't have Tommy Tinker. They surely do now!

 *Crystal Wood*

Kitty Kwips

Kama-Kamille-Kitty: Salem is a chameleon. She was a black Colorado kitty, yet when we moved to the Texas heat, she changed color! We have no idea what spurred it—we thought perhaps the heat—but suddenly she was a beautiful light gray. It changed back to black after about six months. Funnily enough, her coat has done this several times as we've moved, but it always changes back to black. We've got pictures of her both ways and could easily fool friends that we have two different cats. I like to think that one reason she changes color is because it gives her a bit of a blue merle look, so she's in keeping with our merle Aussie, Lindy, whom she adored. Because she considers herself a puppy, she probably thinks of herself as a Kaussie (Aussie kitty) and likes having Aussie markings. Plus, this camouflage enabled her to blend right in with her big brother, Lindy, when she cuddled with him. -*Mimi Gifford*

Kizzy Gizzy Lizzy: Someone threw a two- or three-week-old kitten over my fence, which I found underneath my deck. I took the kitten into the house and saw she was a beautiful calico. Her face was split right down the middle, part black and part gold. We named her Gizmo, and later called her Gizzy Lizzy. I bottle fed her and always kissed her. As she grew up, she loved kissing us while we were sleeping. That little sandpaper tongue would wake us right up. No matter where we sat, Gizzy Lizzy would be on our shoulders trying to give or get a kiss. -*Holly Allen*

Love Lost and Found

We all know the story. Girl meets boy. Girl rejects boy. Girl realizes boy is perfect. But by then, is it too late?

Art: Look Into My Blue Eyes

Oh, there's someone looking at me. Pick me, pick me! I'm beautiful; look at my glossy black-and-white coat. I have unusual sea-blue eyes, and I want to be your lap kitty. Oh, oh no, she's walking by. Wait, come back! I want to be yours.

She's still looking! Oh no, not the loud one in the corner, I'll be quiet. I'll be yours forever. Please come back. Here she comes! No. There she goes.

Lisa: The First Day of Looking

Look at all the cats. There are so many beautiful, wonderful babies who need homes. How can I pick just one? There's a beautiful Maine Coon in the corner, but no, she talks too much. I know that someone so beautiful will find a home. There's one male, check. Healthy coat and eyes—incredible sea blue, in fact. Check. Black-and-white tuxedo, no. Too much like the one I just lost. I can't get one who looks just like Ma Ma Kitty.

Art: A Week Later

Look who's back! It's the person from last week. She has to notice me today. She's going back to that noisy one in the corner. Geez, you know, beauty is only skin deep. Wait, she's coming back and looking at *me*! Purrr, mew, pick me! She is! Oh yes, let's sit and stare into each other's eyes, I'll show you just how much I want a new home and how great we can be together. And she's brought another human with her. Maybe he'll talk some sense into her. What? You're not taking me home with you? I can be the kitty of your dreams. Just let me prove it to you.

Lisa: That Same Day

I remember him. The blue eyes are stunning. Oh, listen! He is trying to get my attention. Ok, little guy. Yes, we can sit together and chat. You even like to rub noses. My, you don't even want to get down. You know a sucker when you see one, huh? Oh, your coat is so smooth and you are so cuddly. Maybe, just maybe, you're the one. "Honey what do you think of him?"

Lisa: Three Days Later

Today is the day; I know just who I want. So much consideration in picking the right one. We've talked and thought about this, and we know who will fit into our lives and laps. Now, we just hope he's still there. To make things better, Oren has a favorite, and I can get her, too!

Art: New Day—No Visitors

Where is that person whose lap I sat in last week? She was so nice, petting me like I was a king. Wait, *yes*! There she is. I've been waiting for you! YES! She's stopping, and what's that she is telling the worker? I'm going home!

Art: A Few Hours Later

Yikes, what is that white thing? He smells funny and makes weird noises. I guess he's what the others in the shelter call a dog. I hope he realizes that I am here to be king. And there's another cat—a girl. Okay, I hear ya; you're the queen, which means there is room for a king. A place just for me.

Lisa: The Next Day

We've decided to call him Art. Well, really Art Vandelay, like the Seinfeld character. He has a room for himself until he gets use to Marris and Ted. A new litter box, squeaky toys, and cat nip. I know that he has to acclimate to the house and vice versa, but I can't wait until he can spend all his time with us. I have never had a cat so engaging and loving. He wants to be in my lap all the time and purrs like a Mustang GT motor. What a great kitty, and such a beautiful one, too. How did we get so lucky?

Art: One Week Later

Uh oh, mom seems sad. What's happened? What does it mean that she's lost her job? Does this mean that I have to go back? Is she giving me up like the other people did?

Lisa: A Bad Day

Oh Artie, it's not a good day. There are changes at work and they don't want me anymore. I wonder if that's how you felt when your first humans gave you to the shelter? It hurts when someone tells you that you aren't good enough, doesn't it? Don't worry, my little one. You and I will make the best of this. You know what it means, don't you? We can spend all our time together, not just at night when I am tired and stressed out. A little quality time for all of us won't be such a bad thing after all. This gives us plenty of time to get to know each other and have some fun!

Art: Today

I've been sick a lot. Nothing that Mom and the vet can't help me with, but there are some days when I just feel sick. Mom makes me take bad-tasting white pills. I try to show her who's boss, but she always wins somehow. She and dad always tell me that I'm lucky they picked me; they know someone else may not have been able to help me so much. Trust me, I'm grateful!

So many changes have happened. Ted, my dog-brother, crossed over to a place where he isn't old and tired anymore. There's another cat, Pookie, the orange terror. I mean he's fun and all; it's just that he can be a brat. And then there's that big golden one. She is quiet and never barks, but man, is that tail scary. She can swat me in the face and never even know it. I keep my distance from her!

Hey wait, Mom's home! Sit down Mom; sit down. I can't wait to sit in your lap. Oh yes, the chair that lays back. I can crawl on your chest and make room for Queen Marris and my little brother Pookie, too. Purrrph, purrph. This is heavenly.

Lisa: Today

Hey Artie, how did all of you do today? Did you get to sleep in the sun? Of course, we'll sit down and share the evening together. You know that I love you all and can't wait to hold you close and pet your soft coats. We'll make room for the others, too. You know there's enough love for everyone.

You knew how to play the game, didn't you Artie? You waited patiently for me to realize you were the man, or rather, the cat, for me. How lucky for all of us!

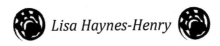 *Lisa Haynes-Henry*

First Meeting

This week I got a new kitten named Whisper. He is cream-colored with dark ears, tail, and feet. His name is Whisper because his meow is very sparse. So far we have some minor—nothing major—problems. We have another cat whose name is Wiley. Wiley is an immense gray Ragdoll cat with white paws. It was hard to predict what would happen when they met; Wiley hissed and lurched at Whisper. His hiss was intense, and it petrified little Whisper.

When we first brought Whisper home, he went to investigate his new urban house. The first night was a disaster, as he tried to flee. He ran under my bed and wanted to stay there all night. The next day he finally came out to play. He climbed my ladder to the top bunk bed and toppled back down to the ground. It was lucky he didn't fracture his foot. Whisper is really cool!

 *Brennen Forman, 5th grade*

Saved by a Kitty and the Internet

It is hard to believe that the big, lovable man-cat we call Boris came to us only five short years ago. It feels like he has always been here, a part of this family and my best friend.

When he came to us, he was such a little thing that he could fit in the palm of our hands with room left over. He appeared on our doorstep when a neighbor and her boyfriend came knocking with a cookie tin in hand. Instead of cookies, that tin held a small kitten that the neighbor's boyfriend had found while cleaning out a shed with his grandfather.

The neighbors had come to ask the crazy cat ladies if we wanted a kitten. We already had three senior cats in our house, and we really felt it was not a good time to bring a kitten into the household. We declined.

As the kids walked away, we heard one of them say, "We'll take it down to the humane society." Knowing full well what the humane society would do to a tiny kitten who needed to be hand-fed, I stopped them in their tracks. The first thought that went through my mind was that the shelter would put him down, and there was no way I was letting that happen. I quickly made the decision that we would take care of the kitty until we could find a place for him.

Since I knew absolutely nothing of hand-raising a kitten, I turned to the Internet for help, which is where I found a group that pointed me to a kitten rescue website. Without their help, I don't know what I would have done. All I know is that I was not going to give up on this kitten.

That's the story of how, with the help of the Internet, we rescued a white-and-gray tabby kitten, whom we soon named Boris. Little did I know that one day Boris would return that favor.

From the time he was finally allowed to be loose in the house, he would greet me at the back door whenever I came home from work. No matter how hard my day was, he always came running when he heard that back door open, and my spirits would lift. In fact, Boris' backdoor greeting still has the same effect on me five years later.

Back then I would call, "Hey, Squirt," and he would pick up his pace before wrapping himself around my feet and legs until I would reach down and scoop him up into my arms. Now, as an adult cat of nearly 25 pounds, we continue with our ritual. Although it is a little harder for me to scoop him up now, I still do. However, I have replaced the term of endearment I used when he was but a wee little squirt to a more suitable, "Hey, Moose!"

When Boris was two, my partner and I were in an automobile accident. While Beth was only bruised, I was hospitalized for a few days with six broken ribs. When I returned home, I was met with my usual greeting, but somehow Boris knew I could not reach down and pick him up. He followed me into the living room where I was to spend the next three weeks recuperating on the sofa.

Never once did Boris leave my side. He was always there right next to me on the sofa or on the blanket down by my feet. Night and day he watched over me and nursed me back to health. He was my furry little nursemaid.

After the accident, I went through a bout of depression. Every day without fail Boris would greet me as usual. Each day it seemed as if there was just a little more spring in his steps, as if he was telling me to cheer up because he was here now, and everything was going to be okay. Soon enough it was.

But his biggest challenge was yet to come.

My mom had a stroke the day after Christmas the following year. She died a few days later and was buried on New Year's Eve. By March my dad had become so depressed, confused, and physically ill that he had to be hospitalized a few days before my birthday. Being hospitalized was not helping him. In fact, his doctor was telling us he should be allowed to starve himself if that is what he wanted. He kept telling us that we should just let him go.

This was all starting to really affect me, and it was showing in my behavior. I was staying up all night and not eating properly. All I did was go to work and spend the nights on Facebook. It was brought to my attention that my behavior on that popular social networking site was becoming a little bizarre, and perhaps I needed some help. I did seek professional help, but at the same time I also took steps to help myself.

Late one night I was online, and Boris was on the sofa beside me looking up at me with those big green eyes. He seemed to be asking me what he could do to help. At that moment a crazy thought went through my head, and I went about setting up a Facebook profile for him. His new Facebook page was a great outlet for all the stress that was building up inside me.

The Facebook profile soon led to a Twitter (another popular social networking site) account, where his personality blossomed. I could truly lose myself in this fantasy animal world of cats and dogs on the net. By becoming Boris online, I was able to deal better with my real life issues.

Boris pulled me out of a very dark place when I needed him the most. It was his turn to rescue me.

Later I saw a bumper sticker that read, "Who rescued who?" This has since become our motto. Boris and I are trying to give back to the world by using his internet voice to help other homeless pets in need.

 *Kelly Hoffman*

Heaven Sent

It was a cold and wet November morning in Phoenix when I first saw her; soaked and obviously scared, she hid beneath the bumper of my car as I offered her a plate of dry food. It took two weeks, but I finally coaxed her to my front door, where I offered her the shelter of a cardboard box lined with a soft, dry towel and fresh food and water each day. I'd only recently lost my cat, Chili-Mac, and had decided my heart couldn't take another beating, so I'd refused to let another fur-baby in. As Thanksgiving approached I called everyone I knew asking if they'd take this little girl in, but no one was interested.

Angry with God for letting this poor, helpless creature suffer, I did the only thing I could—I took her in for a night (only one night, I swore to myself). She slept the entire night on my chest as I lay on the living room sofa, in and out of sleep, still angry with God.

The next morning I put her in a box and drove to the Arizona Humane Society to turn her in. Much to my surprise and dismay, they were full, so they directed me to the Maricopa County Animal Services, where I knew she'd be put to death.

As I left the Humane Society office still holding the box, I sobbed. I remember actually yelling at God: "Why can't you find a home for this one sweet, little cat?"

And then I heard His answer, as clearly as I hear my fingers typing on this keyboard: "She *is* home."

I drove straight to my veterinarian and asked him to check her over and do whatever it took to ensure her health and well-being. He asked, "What's her name?"

"Angel," I said. "It has to be Angel. She's a gift from God."

Angel shared heart and hearth with me for 14 wonderful years, and in many ways, she brought me back to life. Her love was as much a gift as she herself was. And I thank God for every blessed day I had with my sweet Angel.

Lori Lamb

Kitty Kwips

Mine: When we went to the humane society to get a cat, my husband wanted me to look at a five-year-old Himalayan. Mocha was very playful and friendly, but I wasn't sure I was ready to commit. While I looked around at the other cats, another person picked up Mocha and said, "Gross," throwing her back into her cage. Poor Mocha had a horrible hack-job-of-a-haircut due to neglect and also had tear stains underneath her eyes. Additionally, she was underweight, but that person really didn't have to *throw* her back into the cage! Right then I said, "Don't touch her. She is ours, and we are taking her home with us today," and she has been the perfect cat ever since. -*Lindsey & Tim Ware*

Guardian Angel: I fostered Miracle, a very small, sick kitten, but didn't really understand the meaning of her name until one special day. As she grew into a strong, healthy cat, she always slept on a heating pad in a box at night. One morning, after she had gotten out of her box, she ran back to it meowing frantically and scratching at her blanket. I checked to see what was wrong and discovered that the heating pad had overheated and was about to catch fire. Of course, I took the pad out, but I think if she hadn't let me know something was wrong, my house would have caught fire! I am so thankful for *my Miracle*, a guardian angel to this 81-year-old lady who lives alone. -*Addie Peacock*

Freckles' Friends

I was a volunteer at a local animal shelter where I met my special cat, Freckles. During my time there, I saw so many wonderful animals in need of homes. I must admit I have a soft spot for old, sick, and special needs animals, as I would notice how often they were overlooked by potential adopters. Most people only want cute, healthy, young puppies or kittens, and so they pass by those with health issues or missing limbs.

Freckles was about ten years young. Shortly after she arrived at the shelter, she developed ringworm so bad that it nearly killed her. She lost all the hair on her entire body, except for a little on the top of her head. She was so ill and depressed that we were all worried she would not make it. After months of medical treatment, which consisted of daily medical baths, oral meds, and no human touch, she finally started to pull through. We could touch her as long as we wore gloves, but it really was not the same. She was so sweet and loving, and all she really wanted was to be held.

I spent hours sitting in front of Freckles' cage talking to her, telling her that I would adopt her, but she needed to get better first. Once she finally pulled through, I kept my promise to her. Freckles finally came home with me, and there she met her new brothers and sisters: my other cats, a dog named Lexi, and pet mice who were all rescued. Freckles made herself right at home. She had a unique friendship with Sebastian, a red mouse. Abby, another rescue cat, Freckles, and Sebastian would all nap together.

Freckles was so laid back and gentle that I could take her anywhere. Anyone who knows cats knows they generally don't readily accept change. Not only did Freckles love going to others' homes, she loved riding in the convertible with the top down, stretched out in her bed and catching a few rays from the sun. Sometimes she would look out the window, and I loved seeing other driver's reactions to my *cat* in the car! People would laugh that a cat could be so easygoing.

Freckles' main objective was to entertain people wherever she went. Because of her great personality, Freckles became a therapy cat for the elderly in nursing and assisted living homes. She brought smiles to everyone there, even those who had not smiled recently. Some elderly people had not spoken words in years, but when Freckles came, they would ask to hold her. She always obliged.

Shortly after adopting Freckles, she was diagnosed with diabetes, which required insulin twice daily. All my friends are animal lovers, so they understood. If we made dinner plans, we had to go around Freckles' insulin schedule.

Freckles loved going to PetSmart and sitting in the cart to view all the birds, mice, rats, dogs, and other cats needing homes. She always made friends everywhere she went. Freckles learned to wave, which really made people smile. Her coat finally grew back to a shiny black with white underneath, black feet with white socks, and on the socks were black freckles, hence her name, Freckles.

Freckles continuously made me laugh, sleeping with me on a high pile of pillows, where she propped herself and didn't move all night long. She lived with me for five years before her diabetes got the best of her. I lost four animals in one month, all on Fridays: Freckles, Abby, Sebastian, and Lexi all died one week apart from each other. It was one of the worst months ever, but never a day goes by where I don't think of my furry friends and smile. Freckles made my life so much richer and happier.

I still continue to adopt special needs animals. Some don't live very long, but the time we have together is rewarding and makes the heartache of losing them worthwhile.

 *Robin Robichaud*

The Cat in the Box

When my daughter was seven, we went to see our friend Tony who owned a pet store. He didn't sell puppies or kittens. Tony sold fish, mice, birds, hamsters, pet food, and supplies. People would often leave kittens and puppies at his back door, but Tony wouldn't sell them; he found them homes.

We always went in Tony's back door, but this time a box was right in front of the door. We took the box inside, and when we opened it, we saw a very small, scared black-and-white cat. Also in the box was a bill from a vet in New Jersey on which someone had written a note saying he or she couldn't keep the cat. The owner's name was crossed out, and when I called the vet, he would not divulge any information.

My daughter helped Tony in his store that day, and when she came home, she brought the little cat in her sweater pocket. We named the cat Mittens because she had four white feet. She never liked to be picked up and would growl and hiss. We think she was dropped or maybe the box she arrived in had been dropped with her inside it.

We didn't know it then, but Mittens was pregnant with four kittens. When the kittens were about four weeks old, my Aunt Toot came to visit. Aunt Toot didn't like cats because when she was young, someone had thrown a cat at her, and as could be expected, she got scratched. Nevertheless, one by one, Mittens deposited the kittens between Aunt Toot's feet, and Aunt Toot didn't object. I believe Mittens was showing off her little family.

Mittens' kittens were all different: one black, one gray striped, one brown marble, and one gray and white. They were so cute, and Mittens was a great mommy. When the kittens were nine weeks old, we found homes for them, and Mittens was spayed.

Years went by, and my daughter moved out. Then I moved to another state and brought Mittens with me. While living in the South, Mittens was a great hunter of bugs and lizards. Any intruder in the house was fair game for Mittens.

I later moved back to my home state with Mittens, who was an old girl by then. Though a small, now toothless, indoor cat, Mittens still could keep the house dogs away. She wasn't afraid of anything. Because she was so tough, we used to call her Mittens Magee from Jersey. Mittens always loved to be petted, but watch out if you tried to pick her up. She lived to be 21 and was a wonderful girl all along. She passed on four years ago, but we miss Mittens still, and in our hearts we have a special place for the cat in the box.

 *Holly Allen*

Life is Good

Hi, my name is Meesha. I am a beautiful, petite Siamese-mix kitty. My foster mommy also calls me Mommy, Mama, or Mimi. But before I had these sweet names and a wonderful mommy, I was nameless, homeless, and beset by tragedy.

I was born somewhere in Kentucky. The person who found me considered keeping me, until they found out I was pregnant. I had six babies: three girls and three boys. They were all so cute! All were Siamese-looking like me, except for one female who was black and white. But the people no longer wanted us, so they took my babies and me to the local shelter. We remained at the shelter for several weeks, and due to overcrowded conditions, we were all set to be euthanized. That is, until a wonderful group from Pennsylvania heard about us and decided to rescue us.

One by One Cat Rescue arranged to bring us up to Pennsylvania and help find us homes. Our trip started with a hop from one Kentucky shelter to another for a few days. There we received feline leukemia and FIV tests and got our first set of shots. Once our test results came back negative, we were cleared to take our trip to Pennsylvania!

It was a 10-hour trip in a small crate, but it was worth it to be given a chance to live! Once we got to Pennsylvania, we met our foster mommy, Shelly. She gave us a nice big room all to ourselves, with a large window through which we could watch the birds. We had a big cat tree to climb and soft, fluffy beds to curl up in. It was *heaven*! Life was looking good and everything was going to be okay. Until three days later...

One night, Mommy noticed that one of my baby girls seemed lethargic and dehydrated. She planned on getting her into the vet the next morning, but my kitten passed away during the night. Mommy found her curled up with all her siblings, right before noticing that one of my boys was sick, too, and struggling to walk. We were all rushed to the vet, where my boy sadly had to be euthanized because he was too far gone.

We spent the next 24 hours at the vet, with all test results coming back negative. My babies' deaths were shrouded in mystery, and I remained very sad.

The next day we all went home. Mommy still feared that a third kitten was sick, as he just didn't seem right. Unfortunately her fears were realized the next morning, when a second of my boys had passed away overnight, and again, a fourth kitten appeared sick. Another emergency trip to the vet ended in tragedy, when my third and last son had to be euthanized. This time the diagnosis came quickly—feline panleukopenia—*distemper*. My remaining two girls had it, too. They were quickly rushed to an emergency care clinic where they had their best chance at survival. I wasn't showing symptoms, so I stayed at the original vet's office all alone, not knowing if I would ever see my girls again. I didn't know what was happening. Life seemed to have been getting good. What was going on? Why?

Miraculously, my two girls survived. We were reunited two days later back at Mommy's house. I was *very* happy to see them! I gave them a bath and told them I loved them. *Now* it would be okay.

Days passed, and my girls got healthier and healthier. Soon it was like nothing was ever wrong. A few weeks later, it was time for them to be big girls and leave the nest. They now live together with their new family in Collegeville, Pennsylvania, where they will remain together forever.

As for me, I am still at home with Mommy. We are working with the vet on getting me completely healthy, as I was emaciated and weak when I first came here. My babies had taken a toll on my body, and though I didn't have distemper, I, too, was struggling to survive. I have some digestive problems that we will hopefully straighten out soon. I'm not sure if I will stay with Mommy forever, as I understand she is just my foster Mommy. But regardless, I know that I will be just fine, as Mommy has promised me a fantastic home no matter what.

I will always miss my babies, but I know that I will see them all again someday in heaven. And *now* everything really *is* okay, and life is good.

 Meesha, Translated by Shelly Nowotarski

Kitty Kwips

Well-Placed Trust: A pregnant chocolate point Siamese became our daily visitor when we moved into a new home. Before long the visits ceased, but then one day I came home from work to find five beautiful kittens on my front porch; Mama was nowhere to be found, but she apparently trusted me enough to care for her babies. These five- or six-week-old kittens obviously had had zero socialization with humans. I scooped them up and gave them the guest bathroom where they could temporarily reside and romp. This was pure joy. It didn't take long to find good homes for all five. Four went to live with others, and I kept the tuxedo kitten. My daughter commented on the kitten's purr factor and suggested we name her Chevie after our car. *Purr*fect. Chevie is the only cat we've known who will actually chase sponge balls and retrieve them. She is a total joy! -*Andi Anderson*

Daily Delights: Sissy was anything but a sissy, but that was the name she had when I adopted her. Sissy had two habits that were absolutely a delight to me. **Delight #1:** Every morning when I finished my shower, Sissy hid around the corner, waiting for me to walk through the door. She then jumped up and wrapped herself around my leg, hanging on until I reached the bedroom to dress. Fortunately, she had been declawed by the previous owners... **Delight #2:** (Keep in mind I live on the 29th floor where the balcony railing ran clear around the building.) After her breakfast, Sissy would take a stroll by hopping up on the rail and walking clear around the building. She would reappear about 15 minutes later. My neighbors got quite a kick out of seeing Sissy walk by their balcony, sometimes dropping in for a short visit. -*Charlie Heckathorn*

Marley and her four littermates were living in a back yard, their feral mama cat still nursing them and teaching them to hunt. When the kittens were old enough to leave their mom, I gathered them up with the help of the homeowner, and off to the vet we went. To my utter horror, all five kittens, only eight weeks old, tested positive for FIV (*feline immunodeficiency virus, also known as feline AIDS*). The vet recommended euthanizing all five kittens.

I had a limited understanding of FIV, but I couldn't imagine this was the only option for five beautiful, active, otherwise healthy babies. I took them home and started researching the disease. Most of the information I found stated that kittens would outgrow it. So for 30 days I took care of the brood.

Marley stood out from the very beginning. She had so much personality and no fear. She greeted my 100-pound dog without hesitation, insisting on grooming him and sleeping with him, tucked as close to his tummy as possible and nestled between his long legs. Marley greeted everyone who visited our home. She would chirp along with the human conversation and move from person to person.

Sure enough, after 30 days, all five kittens tested *negative* for FIV. I was able to find adopters for a pair of the kittens, leaving me with Marley plus two. Then an adopter came along for another pair, which left me with Marley. It was meant to be.

Two years after adopting Marley, my 10-year-old dog, Bubba, the love of my life, passed away very suddenly. Marley has been my comfort. She is so in-tune, so perceptive, and so nurturing; she knew our home had lost a family member and that Mom was in pain. She is an amazing cat; I have known no other like her. She is hours of entertainment, chasing lights, perching atop the coat rack, lounging above the kitchen cabinets, and chirping at the birds through the window. I love her dearly.

As I have continued to rescue homeless cats and provide them a foster home, Marley is the ultimate host and mentor. She sits quietly with the feral cats recovering from their spay or neuter, providing them with comfort and boosting their confidence. She interacts more than usual with everyone when the skittish kitties are in view, and she is the immediate best friend and caretaker to the incoming kittens and cats who are just waiting for a family to call their own. That's my Marley—a one-of-a-kind cat with a heart of gold.

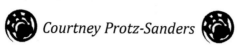 *Courtney Protz-Sanders*

Baby in a Blanket

"Oh, my God! It's a cat, and he's alive!"

That's exactly what I said to myself as I passed a small black lump of fur lying five feet from the busy highway. I was traveling in the city, going 55 M.P.H. in bumper-to-bumper rush hour traffic, yet I made eye contact with that terrified, injured feline. He was surrounded by nothing but cement: highway, shoulder, and sound barrier.

It probably took me only 10 minutes to turn around, backtrack, and park my car on an entrance ramp, but it felt like an eternity. I was so afraid the cat would bolt into traffic and be killed before I could rescue him.

Since it was a hot August afternoon, I left the car running with the air conditioner blasting and my purse on the passenger's seat. (Yes, I know. But when an animal is at risk, I sort of lose my sensibility!) Before heading for the highway, I grabbed a blanket to protect both of us because I had no idea how badly my feline friend was injured.

At first I thought he was gone, but I had simply misjudged the distance from the ramp to where he lay curled up. When I finally spotted him, I stopped and began to quietly talk to him. He looked at me with huge yellow eyes filled with pain and fear. Ever so slowly I inched forward, closing the gap between us. I prayed that the cars streaming by would not honk their horns or otherwise spook him. Finally, after what felt like a lifetime, he made a slight movement toward me. I had gained his trust! I closed the distance between us ever so carefully, talking in a soothing voice the whole while. As I gently picked him up and put the blanket over him to block out the traffic, he buried his head in my arms.

It wasn't over yet, however. We still had a long walk to the safety of my car. I kept up the quiet dialogue, telling him everything was going to be okay. To my amazement, a gentle soul pulled over on the exit ramp and gave us a ride to my car. She mistook me for a homeless person with a baby, but hey, I needed something to laugh about in order to break the tension. Imagine her surprise when I showed her the cat in my blanket!

Freeway has been a part of our family since that steamy August day four years ago. Most of his injuries were minor, yet painful. His claws were worn down so badly from trying to scale the sound barrier wall that we thought he was declawed. His pads were scratched and scraped, and one of his teeth was chipped. His worst injury, a broken hip, required surgery, from which he recovered quickly.

One would think that Freeway would act like a pet who is forever indebted to his family for rescuing him and giving him a home. You might imagine him gazing lovingly into our eyes as we hold him in our laps. Yeah, right. To be fair, I am sure he is grateful, but he definitely has "cattitude." He is Alpha Kitty, ruling the roost and accepting our love and cuddles only when it suits him. After all, he is a cat!

 *Sara Linker Nord*

The Tennessee Shuffle

I t was time. I had put down my best buddy Nete due to renal failure.

Three years later I was ready for another feline—a black one, of course. On to Petfinder.com, where I was certain I would quickly find the cat or kitten who was hoping I'd stumble on to him or her.

Distance from home wasn't important. I would drive wherever necessary to adopt my kitty guy or gal. And there he was at a shelter in Cookeville, Tennessee: Lenny. He looked so forlorn, like he'd given up hope of gaining his forever home. I quickly paid the $65.00 fee via Paypal and called the shelter to inquire when I could rescue him.

The next day I took off of work and drove the 125 miles to pick up Lenny. Imagine my dismay when I arrived at the shelter to find they had already adopted him out the day before! The shelter director assured me that Lenny would be retrieved and delivered to me the next day. Sure enough, the following evening a volunteer met me with a cat in a restaurant parking lot.

Because it was dark, I didn't get a good look at the cat until I got him home. To my shock, he was *not* Lenny! It was a black kitten for sure, but it wasn't Lenny. I could have caused a stink, but since this kitten was lively, mischievous, and could really belt out a song, I decided not to even call the shelter. After all, it appeared Lenny had also found a home.

So, I changed this cat's name to Joseppi, and he has been the love of my life ever since.

 *Andi Anderson*

Catrobat

G ene and I were in the car going up a hill near our house, when we saw a young black-and-white tuxedo cat lying in the road. Gene got out of the car and went over to it. He looked and thought, "The cat is dead." Then he looked again and thought the same thing. But something made him look a third time, which is when he saw the cat breathe.

We shifted the cat onto a pillow we had in the car and took him to the emergency vet. He started to revive and cry out on the way there. We left him at the vet's office, where it was thought that he had probably run into the side of a car or its tire and got knocked out. Then we went back to that neighborhood and looked for an owner, but no one said they knew him. People said there were lots of homeless cats in the neighborhood. We looked in the newspaper, too, for a while, but no one put in a notice looking for him. The vet said not to look too hard because the cat was blind, and the vet believed a blind cat would be soon abandoned. The cat nevertheless seemed to have a sixth sense about not falling off the vet's examination table. Well, we named him Bon Chance (good luck), Chance for short, because he was lucky we saw him. If he had stayed in the road much longer, a car most likely would have killed him. After a few days, six-month-old Chance recovered his sight. From that time on, Chance was a talker and a daredevil, who liked to stick out his tongue as he slept.

When Chance was still young, we found a small lump on his back, so we took him to the vet who had neutered him. A new vet had been hired to help the regular vet, and we ended up seeing him. He felt the lump, told us it was probably cancer, and said we should put Chance to sleep. Fortunately, Gene and I decided that vet was an idiot, and we took Chance to another vet across town. That vet operated and took out the BB pellet which was lodged under the skin of Chance's back. Years later, a neighbor's daughter let slip that her father sometimes shot BB pellets at cats if they wandered into his garden. (Who knew! The man seemed nice in every way.)

Chance was a cat who liked heights. Sometimes he would climb so far up a tree in the back yard that I didn't see how he could ever climb down, but he did. He also liked to get into a round plastic tub, so I could carry him around on my head. Chance would feign interest in everything I brought near him, always looking and sniffing.

When we did some major remodeling of the house, Chance was there. Everywhere. He was under the house in the crawl space and also in the eaves and the rafters, tightrope walking on beams. He would get on the porch railing and then jump onto the roof. He loved lying at the peak of the roof. If we drove up, he would lazily lift his head, look over the peak to see who it was, and then go back to sleep. Even though he could get down by himself, Chance trained me to come outside with a stool when he called to me. I would hold the stool up, he would get on it, and I would lower him off the roof.

When I painted the outside of our house, I was up on a ladder near the peak of the roof with bees flying around my head. Chance didn't care, he came right up that ladder with me, and fortunately we didn't fall. Another time, a neighbor left a ladder leaning against his house, and Chance used it to climb onto the man's roof. The man didn't want Gene or me on his roof because of the potential liability, so he climbed up and approached Chance while clapping his hands (he had a dog and probably thought it a friendly thing to do). I clap my hands to discourage cat fighting and what I consider bad behavior, so Chance promptly jumped off the man's roof and onto the ground. He appeared entirely unhurt, but we probably should've taken him to the vet anyway just to be sure.

When I brought JJ, a homeless orange tabby, home, he soon bit Chance and gave him an abscess. He tried to drive Chance off. It was only by the merest chance that I realized what was going on. I went down the street, picked up Chance, and brought him home. After that, one would go outside, and one would come inside. A few years later, when they both went to the vet to have their teeth cleaned, I forgot to tell the vet not to put them in the same cage. When I called, they told me both Chance and JJ were indeed in the same cage, huddled together, united against the world.

Chance lived with us for 15 years.

Perhaps the young vet we had visited so many years before and whose advice we had rejected was a fortune teller. A couple of years before he died, Chance developed a cyst on his back. The vet said I could sterilize a needle and drain the cyst when it became large, so I did. We went on like this for a couple of years. I dearly loved Chance and consequently had tried to do everything that seemed right to prolong his life, which included regular vaccinations with the distemper combo shot and a rabies vaccine. I believe that Chance's cyst and eventual cancer originated at the vaccination site, and now I no longer give our cats those combo shots after the first couple of times. I have read that many now believe those initial shots confer lifetime immunity. The vet I currently use gives the rabies vaccine in the back leg (it is legally required in my state), so if the cat develops cancer at the shot site, the leg can be amputated and the cat's life saved.

Chance was clearly dying, and I couldn't bear to euthanize him or to see him suffer, so we let the vet open him up and try to remove the cancer as a last resort. The evening before the operation, I offered Chance a plate of the cantaloupe pieces he loved. He sniffed them and purred and purred, but he was too sick to eat. Unfortunately, when he was opened up the vet discovered that the cancer had spread throughout Chance's organs. The vet stitched Chance up, though still anesthetized, and brought him out for me to say goodbye. Then he gave Chance the needles to end his life.

Chance stuck out his tongue as he died. The vet seemed disturbed by this, but although devastated, I took it as a sign that things were all right.

 *Sarah Qualman*

Hole in the Wall

I arrived at my downtown office one Monday morning and parked in the area behind the building that houses many small offices and, at the time, a family-owned restaurant. The owner of the restaurant was standing out beside her back door with a worried expression on her face. She hurried up to me as I got out of my car. "You can help?" she asked in broken English, pointing and waving toward a small vent in the outside wall of the building. "Cat—in there!"

I raced over to the vent, which was partially covered by an ancient cast-iron grate. Listening intently, I finally heard what had alerted the restaurant owner—a tiny meow in the dark space beyond the grate. There was barely enough room for me to get my arm through, but I reached in and pulled out one small, black, scruffy kitten, less than a month old. He was dirty, and his eyes were swollen and glued shut with infection, but he hissed and fought against his giant captor like a panther! I quickly felt around in his hiding place, but there were no other kittens. Lacking anything better, I placed him in a file box and hurried him to our family vet.

I was afraid this scrawny specimen was beyond help, but the vet cleaned his eyes and gave him antibiotics. When the kitten was offered a bottle of kitten milk replacer, he gulped it down greedily.

"Are you going to keep him?" the vet asked. At the time, I wasn't sure what his fate would be, so I just shrugged. The vet said, "Well, he's got to have a name for the record. What do you want to call him?"

I thought for a minute and then said, "I pulled him out of a wall, so his name is... Wally!" Having named him, I now owned him, and so I brought him home. He needed bottle feeding for about a week but quickly transitioned to solid food. He grew up to be a big, sleek, beautiful black cat with a sprinkling of white hairs around his neck and shoulders. (I call that his "sugar.") He sometimes forgets he's no longer a feral cat and behaves badly, but most of the time he's my special rescued boy.

 *Crystal Wood*

Believe in Miracles

"Please, please! I promise you won't even know I have two!"
I begged with eyes tearing. I was 19.

Mylandlordswerelandscapingoutsidemyapartment on a hot summer afternoon. The husband was an older, weathered man with a kind face. His wife was prim and proper and obviously annoyed. She looked at me with a stern gaze and said, "Young lady, you are lucky we allow you to have one cat; most apartments don't allow any. No."

I turned immediately to her husband with a pleading look. He looked down at the tulips and said softly, "Well now, I don't think I could sleep knowing that I separated two sisters."

I barely noticed his wife's horrified look as I gave him a giant bear hug and grabbed my car keys.

I adopted two kittens, Scarlett and Annie. I was told they were the only two in the litter, which was unusual. I named Annie, a stunning orange tabby, after my grandmother. I wanted to give Scarlett a meaningful name as well. I read a story in a magazine about an apartment building that caught fire. Onlookers watched as a stray cat crawled underneath the burning building to save her newborn kittens. One by one, she carefully carried them in her mouth to safety. With each trip, her body burned more, but she kept going until all her babies were out. By that time, she was so severely burned that no one expected her to survive. "She's a miracle," her rescuers said, and they named her Scarlett. I couldn't have known then, but my Scarlett would be a miracle cat, too.

Scarlett is tiny, fearless, and embodies the stereotype of a calico cat. She scaled my shower curtain with ease the first day I brought her home and then tore it to shreds while I slept. On more than one occasion, she broke into the food bag and stuffed herself before purging all over my living room. She was our self-proclaimed neighborhood watch, always abreast of the latest goings-on. If we had visitors, she beat me to the door to see who it was. She'd steal money out of my purse and put it in her water bowl, and she was a bucking bronco in the bathtub. She would get on the counter in order to be eye-level with me and voice her displeasure when she was unhappy. But when I needed her, she would curl up in the crook of my arm and purr like a train. She did everything, good or bad, with gusto. She helped me survive many changes: moving out of my parents' house, college, my first job, and heartbreak. I shared my grief and my happiness with her.

Then one morning I woke up and found her crouched in the corner, and I knew something was terribly wrong. The veterinarian put her on an IV and told me it was pancreatitis; it was unlikely she would survive. It felt like someone hit me in the face with a shovel. Scarlett was my source of strength; I could not remember a memory that she had not been part of in some way. I thought she was invincible. I cried all the way home with an empty cat carrier in my passenger seat.

The veterinarian called me the next morning. I was stunned to hear excitement in her voice as she told me that Scarlett's recovery was nothing short of a miracle. Scarlett was in the hospital for five days, and every evening after work, I sat with her until they closed. She had survived the pancreatitis, but Scarlett's kidney function was abnormal. She was diagnosed with chronic renal failure. The veterinarian estimated that her kidneys were functioning at 25% and cautioned me that her time was limited. She offered the option of euthanasia, and I held Scarlett while she left me to think. We sat quietly and suddenly Scarlett gave me a push with her forehead (her equivalent to a hug). She looked up at me as if to say, "Please, don't give up." In the corner of a tiny exam room, we made a pact that I would not give up on her as long as she was willing to fight.

Back at home I overcame my fear of needles and learned how to give her fluids through a needle under her skin. Every other day we sat together while I administered the fluids that would help her body clean out the toxins that her shriveling kidneys were unable to purge. I researched the latest information on kidney disease and grew in confidence as her advocate. My linen closet was packed with medicines, bags of fluids, IV lines, needles, and every kind of canned cat food on the market. I suppose it sounds like a big sacrifice, but I never thought about it in that way. We were on a journey together, and I was committed to see it through. When I felt overwhelmed, all I had to do was look at her. Scarlett was fighting the real battle; I had it easy.

When my husband and I moved from North Carolina to New York, my veterinarian was reserved. She warned me that a long trip would be taxing on Scarlett's body and that I needed to prepare myself for the possibility that she would not make it. I gave her extra fluids and said a prayer as I loaded her up and drove for 13 hours. It's been three years since we made that trip. Scarlett has been with us through building a new house, new jobs, and my first pregnancy, attentive to me always.

It has been five years now since Scarlett was first diagnosed. It has not been an easy road, but I am so proud of her. I have seen the grim look on the vets' faces as they admit her back into the hospital, but each time she fights back and surprises everyone. Through her courageous fight, I've learned to have hope, even when things seem hopeless. I credit our veterinarians for saving her life, but I have also witnessed that sometimes things happen that defy logic.

Sometimes numbers are just that—numbers. They can't gauge a pet's soul or their willingness to live.

I'm so very glad that I did not decide to euthanize Scarlett based on the numbers from her blood work five years ago because I would have missed five great years of having her in my life. I do realize that she won't be able to fight this battle forever, and someday, when she and I again sit in the corner of a quiet room, she will tell me it is time. But I will have peace knowing that she and I fought together, for each other, and we have a bond that can never be broken.

Thank you, Scarlett, for teaching me to believe in miracles.

 *Mara Burns*

My Special Corner

The area where the outside fence meets a corner of my house holds a special place in my heart—maybe because the sunlight on a particularly nice day hits the grass just right. This is where I can set out my lawn chair and sit most comfortably with my back to the sun, catching its warm rays as I read the books for which I don't normally have time. Even the breeze there is a little different: extra fragrant, extra soft, whispering gently through the leaves of the hibiscus tree directly in front of me. Maybe the fragrance is, in fact, coming from the hibiscus flowers themselves.

But I have yet to mention the most important reason for me to sit in this particular corner. For many years my cat has chosen this corner for snoozing in the sun. I have had this beautiful creature in my back yard for over 16 years, and when she first made her presence known to me, she was probably over two years old. That would make her 18+ years old in the present day.

I'm told that cats, who reign supreme over the kingdom of sleep, actually sleep even more as they get older. Apparently, it's a detriment to their health if they happen to sleep less and cut corners in this regard. So seeking out perfect corners in which to nap, especially on lovely spring days, becomes even more imperative as they age. My cat is hardly an exception to this.

To my jaundiced eye, this cat is absolutely gorgeous to behold. She is completely, irrevocably, indubitably, black—pitch black. She has big yellow eyes that sometimes carry a greenish tinge. When she opens her mouth to yawn, I can see her enormous, razor sharp canines glinting quite ominously, even though she loves me to death. Her teeth sparkle in the sun that graces this corner; they actually deflect the rays, as she yawns right in my face, facing the sun directly.

She sits right across from me, probably making fun of me silently in her head: "That silly girl, reading a boring novel when she could be doing so many more worthwhile things—like taking a nap or lying directly on the sun-warmed grass. She has been with me now for over 16 years and has yet to learn from my example!"

My special corner always lacks something if Midnight happens not to be there. I look up periodically from whatever novel I am reading to catch my cat's eye, and if I suddenly see that she is no longer there, I have to put my reading down and get up to search for her.

Why would I get up? What about the sun's rays, the fragrant breeze, and the hibiscus flowers? Are they not enough to keep me in my comfortable lawn chair, reading the books I never have time for? The answer, dear Reader, is a resounding *no*. Midnight makes this corner what it is, and I believe she knows it. Maybe that's why she always picks out this corner in which to sleep on nice days, when the sun is shining and the birds are singing: to draw me out, to get me to sit in my lawn chair, to force me to forget my busy schedule and take the time to smell the hibiscus.

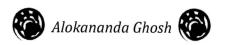 *Alokananda Ghosh*

About Happy Tails Books™

Schnauzer Chihuahua **Golden Retriever** PUG
DACHSHUND German Shepherd Collie **Boxer**
Labrador Retriever Husky Beagle ALL AMERICAN
Border Collie Pit Bull Terrier Shih Tzu Miniature Pinscher
Chow Chow Australian Shepherd Rottweiler Greyhound
Boston Terrier Jack Russell Poodle Cocker Spaniel
GREAT DANE Doberman Pinscher Yorkie SHEEPDOG
ST. BERNARD Pointer Blue Heeler

Happy Tails Books™ was created to help support animal rescue efforts by showcasing the love and joy adopted pets have to offer. With the help of animal rescue groups, stories are submitted by people who have adopted pets, and then Happy Tails Books™ compiles them into books. These books serve not only to entertain but also to educate readers about adoption and the characteristics of each specific breed (when applicable). Happy Tails Books™ donates a significant portion of proceeds back to the rescue groups that help gather stories for the books.

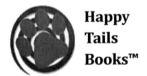

Happy Tails Books™ To submit a story or learn about other books Happy Tails Books™ publishes, please visit our website at http://happytailsbooks.com.